LEARNING AND INCLUSION
The Cleves School Experience

Edited by Priscilla Alderson.
Written by staff and pupils of the
Cleves School, Newham, London

David Fulton Publishers
London

David Fulton Publishers Ltd
The Chiswick Centre, 414 Chiswick High Road, London W4 5TF
www.fultonpublishers.co.uk

First published in Great Britain in 1999 by David Fulton Publishers

Note: The rights of Priscilla Alderson to be identified as the authors of this work have been asserted by them in accordance with the Copyright, Designs and Patents Act 1988.

David Fulton Publishers is a division of Granada Learning Limited, part of Granada plc.

Copyright © Priscilla Alderson 1999

British Library Cataloguing in Publication Data
A catalogue record for this book is available from the British Library.

ISBN 1-85346-609-3

Pages from this book may be photocopied for use only in purchasing institution. Otherwise, all rights reserved. No part of this publication may be reproduced, stored in a retieval system or transmitted, in any form or by any means, electronic, mechanical, photocopying, or otherwise, without the prior permission of the publishers.

Typeset by Textype Typesetters, Cambridge
Printed and bound in Great Britain

Contents

1. Introduction — 1
2. An inclusive community school — 6
3. Active learning — 27
4. Being friends and being equals: relationships and rules — 44
5. Fun — 64
6. The Cleves School experience: conclusion — 73

Appendices:

1. Implementing the aims of Cleves School — 75
2. Extracts from the 1998 OFSTED Report — 79
3. The Newham LEA Inclusion Charter and extracts from the Audit — 84

Bibliography — 90

Chapter 1
Introduction

New challenges to schools can be seen as attempts to stretch schools in opposite and even contradictory directions. The National Curriculum over the past decade has expanded the areas of formal knowledge which children have to learn, and the abilities they have to demonstrate during assessments. Schools are expected to achieve the best possible average results in tests and exams (DfEE 1997a). This can seem to conflict with policies to include every child, of any ability, in mainstream schools (DfEE 1997b). The school day must be highly organised if the curriculum is to be covered. Each primary school teacher must have a breadth and depth of knowledge of many topics. Here, the flow of knowledge is mainly seen as from adults to children. Yet teachers also have to encourage the children's original and questioning thinking, their creativity and social, moral and spiritual awareness. All these flourish in less formal settings, with time to reflect and explore, drawing on children's own ideas rather than 'delivering' education to them. Schools are expected to encourage a strong sense of corporate identity and loyalty yet also to welcome outsiders and newcomers. There are tensions in many school prospectuses between their stated aims that pupils must conform to strict rules and behaviour codes, but also expectations that children will become responsible and independent, able to think critically and to take initiatives (Griffith 1998).

This book describes how one primary school approaches these challenges and works to resolve the tensions in ways that can benefit every child and teacher. Methods of raising standards in one area, such as literacy, behaviour, the inclusion of disabled children, or induction and continuity when new staff and pupils arrive, can work to the benefit of all the other areas.

Facing new challenges

How this book came to be written

Cleves School is widely known about, and referred to by writers on education (Ainscow 1995). In the words of one of the teachers:

> It's very exciting to be here. You're inundated with visitors coming to see what you're doing. I feel proud about what we do and I want to show everybody. The staff I work with are so gifted; when they describe things or reason with the children they're so patient. It is very good practice here. I've worked in a lot of schools, and here it has far wider practices, it's better resourced, well planned.
>
> 'You wouldn't think it would be possible', that's what people say when they come here. To have all the children working alongside profoundly disabled children, and it does work. You see the spin-offs and it would be difficult for me not to work in that way now, it adds another facet to your teaching. I can't think of a good reason to exclude children from their local school. If you are a community school you have to include every member of the family.

Brigid, the head teacher, considers that 'The challenge from the start was to make Cleves an inclusive school. We all believed that this is an ordinary mainstream primary school with nothing special about it.'

This could sound contradictory: an ordinary school which surprises visitors. Cleves School aims to make inclusion ordinary, something which every school can do. Some of the ideas used at Cleves are also popular in other schools but others are more unusual.

The aims of the book

This is not a book about detailed teaching techniques and lesson plans. Instead we aim to:

- describe how Cleves School responds to challenges which other schools also face;
- record ideas and experiences which other schools could find useful to adapt and develop in their own ways; and
- show how the methods of inclusive education and independent and group learning can combine well with methods designed to raise standards of achievement for every child.

The writing committee

A research project was designed for an editor to work with the staff and children on writing a book about their school. The Gatsby Charitable Foundation kindly funded the project. David Fulton and Alison Foyle of David Fulton Publishers visited Cleves and were keen to publish a book about the school.

The writing committee did much of the work from May to July 1998:

Mary, a teacher;
Tanya, a parent governor and temporary clerical assistant;
1998 Year 6 members, Delicia, Harsumeet, Michael, Patrick, Sarah and Sinsi;
with Priscilla from the Institute of Education, University of London.

We would meet in the staff room, make coffee, and then talk about the school and the book. We gradually decided on the chapter headings. We wrote a letter home to every family asking for ideas linked to the chapter headings, and made a book box for people to post in contributions, placed in the school foyer. Deanna, the art specialist, took the photographs. The writing committee did some opinion surveys and also went around the school with tape recorders interviewing people. All the survey and suggestion box comments expressed satisfaction and praised the school. One mother wrote a complimentary poem. To make the book realistic and useful to other schools, we also wanted to report problems and challenges, and how these might be resolved. We asked about problems during individual interviews, and discuss them in the following chapters. One main concern during the summer term was the coming literacy hour, and how its more formal large group methods could fit with Cleves's flexible approach, as shown in Chapter 3.

We would like to have put everyone's names beside their comments, but very often they talked to us in groups, and people agreed a lot; they often seemed to be speaking for many others when they gave their own views. The findings from the surveys supported this. So we decided to record their views in the book without naming all the speakers. 'We' sometimes refers to everyone in the school, sometimes to the staff, and sometimes to the children. Although not everyone will agree with every point, those of us who have checked the drafts of the book think that it fairly reports views generally held in the school. Some of the speakers are named, the main ones are:

Brigid, the head teacher;
Joy, the early years leader;
Debbie, deputy head, SENCO, and curriculum support teacher to early years.

The second stage of writing the book came during the autumn, when drafts were checked and revised. The literacy hour had been introduced in the first week of term, from the reception year onwards. We added sections on how the literacy hour fits, so far, with the other learning activities at Cleves. We are grateful to people who read drafts and gave us critical comments, including Chris Goodey, Linda Jordan, Sarah Martyn and Judy Sebba.

The style of the book

We have aimed for a clear readable style which, we hope, will offer a quick and interesting read for busy teachers. Much of the book records the direct words of the staff and children. Sometimes they spoke about complex ideas, but always in plain English, so that we have not attempted to rewrite their thoughts in more formal terms. We hope that this book conveys something of the experience you would have if you visited the school.

Terms

For reasons which will be shown later, at Cleves the age groups are based in four wings: for early years and reception, ages 3–5 years; for Key Stage 1, Years 1 and 2, ages 6–7 years; for Key Stage 2A, Years 3 and 4, ages 8–9 years; and Key Stage 2B, Years 5 and 6, ages 10–11.

Classes are called base groups and class teachers are base teachers.

The staff work in four teams, each having a senior teacher or team leader and a curriculum support teacher who advises on enabling every child to have access to the curriculum.

The support staff – classroom or welfare assistants and nursery nurseries in every wing – are called learning assistants.

Lessons are called sessions.

The topics through this book

Inclusive education means that every child is welcomed, whatever their degree of disability or learning difficulty, and has full access to the building, the resources and activities in the school. When we opened, it was hard to establish our identity, because then schools were mainly locked into two separate models of special or mainstream schools. Now, all Newham schools include children with special needs, but then it was a challenge to establish a new kind of culture. To overcome the challenge we looked at ways of including everyone through all the daily life of the school. The first way was to set up a differentiated curriculum. Differentiated teaching means teaching all-ability groups and meeting all their different levels at the same time. The second was to use the building in ways that excluded no one – during assemblies, PE, lunch times. We decided not to have playtimes in the morning and afternoon. Instead, we have PE every day in the park, ball games or gymnastics. Chapter 2 describes how, as a community school, Cleves is planned to ensure this access through the design and use of the building and through the team teaching. Chapter 3 explains the methods of active learning and team teaching. Being friends and being equals is considered in Chapter 4, to show how the school setting and activities influence and are influenced by the relationships between everyone working in the school. Chapter 5 shows how relationships link to rules and responsibilities, and Chapter 6 describes the mixtures of work and enjoyment we aim for. Finally, we summarise some of the challenges which, like every primary school, Cleves faces in relation to learning and inclusion. Extracts from some of the policy documents by the school and by Newham Local Education Authority are given at the end of the book.

We hope you enjoy reading about our school

Chapter 2
An inclusive community school

Cleves Primary School is in Newham, East London. As well as being economically one of the most disadvantaged areas of the country, Newham is a lively cosmopolitan area. About ten years ago, Newham Council decided to make improving the education services one of its main priorities. Because of the rising numbers of children in the borough, Cleves School was opened in a new building in September 1992.

We begin by explaining the main aims of the school, and then the ways through which we achieve them.

The aims of our school

These aims have been agreed by the Staff and Governors of Cleves Primary School. They are reviewed annually. We have a shared vision of developing relationships and a curriculum that ensures that everyone feels valued, respected and reaches a high level of achievement.

1. Access to learning

- to provide an environment where each child of every race, gender, class and learning need is truly recognised, accepted and valued;
- to create an environment where there is a place for everyone and there is a feeling of belonging;
- to develop high positive self-esteem in all children and adults;
- to enable children to be aware of their interdependency on each other.

2. Curriculum

- to have an approach to the curriculum that promotes high levels of achievement and which enables children to reach their potential;
- to enable children to have access to and experience of the whole

curriculum, (including the National Curriculum and Religious Education (RE);
- to have a recording and assessment system that demonstrates children's achievement, their development and progression.

3. Process of learning

- to acknowledge that all children are decision makers and to enable them to become active participants in their own learning;
- to enable learning to start from the child's needs;
- to ensure that all the experiences for the children are positive and rigorous;
- to provide a smooth transition from the Early Years to Year 6;
- to prepare children for the transition from Primary to Secondary school successfully and confidently.

(For more details about how our aims are carried out see Appendix 1).

4. Working cooperatively

To ensure that everyone, teachers, children, parents, governors, and other members of the community, works cooperatively and collaboratively to enable the achievement of all.

The children

There is capacity for up to 420 children in the school, and 102 who attend the early years wing, mostly part-time. Cleves is an inclusive mainstream school in an inclusive local education authority (LEA). Newham has closed almost all its special schools. One in ten of the children at Cleves has severe and profound disabilities; in other areas these children would attend schools for severe learning difficulties or residential units.

Over half (53 per cent) of the children are entitled to have free school meals. Much of the local housing is rented, and high rise, and several London boroughs use temporary housing here. Families in Newham move house frequently, so nearly a quarter of the children at Cleves joined the school in the past year. There is a large number of refugees and asylum seekers.

58 per cent of the children at Cleves speak English as an additional language. The children's languages include Urdu, Punjabi, Hindi, Gujarati, Sylheti, Bengali, French, Chinese, Somali, Arabic, Spanish, Portuguese, and a range of African languages. The children who speak English as an additional language are classified for their English speaking as: beginners (13.3%), developing skills (21.8%), extending skills (15%) and fluent (49.9%). Two thirds of the support staff (62%), and 11% of the teachers are of African, Caribbean or Asian origin. We value our children's and staff's bilingual skills. Our governors also represent our diverse community. We do not yet have any disabled staff;

nationally, only 0.1% of teachers were registered as disabled in 1991.

The latest annual attendance figures give clues to how Cleves differs from an average school.

- The national average for authorised absences is 5.0%, and for Cleves is 6.9%. This is partly because some of our children are often ill or in hospital.
- The national average for unauthorised absences is 0.5%, and for Cleves it is 0.1%, a very low rate for inner London primary schools.
- We had no fixed period or permanent exclusions, although, in most other authorities, some of our children with challenging behaviour would attend special schools.

The community

Near the school is West Ham football ground, a large bus garage and a high street mainly of shops selling Asian clothes, fabrics and food. This is a busy area, but there are few free local amenities for children and parents, except a park which has an enclosed children's playground next to the school.

A teacher's comment

> The school is, kind of, the heart of the community. The people living in this area have little else to focus in on. That's very important in the way the school is used by the parents and perceived by the children. It's very much a social place to come to, as well as a place to learn. It is such a beautiful school and the parents and children are proud of it. There's a big waiting list.

Another teacher's comment

> There is a sense that the school is an open place and that people are not blocked off from it so that parents can come in, and many visitors who obviously feel very welcome because they keep coming. When I walk home the children come up and talk to me and we sit and chat in the park so they don't seem to feel that school is isolated from life outside. The parents happily sit talking in the school until 4 o'clock and much later, and they obviously feel they can approach the teachers.

The school joins in community projects. One example is the parade to celebrate the range of autumn festivals associated with light. We make lanterns and join in the procession which ends with fireworks in the park next to the school. Newham schools close on community festival days such as Diwali, Guru Nanak's birthday and Eid-ul-Fitr. In a 'heart stone project', Year 4 surveyed the community around the school for examples of graffiti and racist comments. Their photographs and drawings became part of a display which travelled to Edinburgh and Strasbourg. Another example of links with the community is when children in every age group help the staff in leisure services to plant bulbs in the park.

The welcoming school entrance

Welcome to the school foyer

Our modern building is fully accessible for disabled people and was designed to be used by the community. One way to emphasise that we welcome any child who lives locally is to encourage adults to use the school. As you approach the school, a single level building, you see first the raised glass roof of the foyer. Inside, the foyer is a round light area, with displays of the children's art, a pool of plastic balls to play in, a little house and a large caterpillar tunnel. The foyer leads on to the early years wing, the parents' meeting room and a tea bar for them, the secretary's office, and the corridor to the main part of the school. The strong plastic windows look out on to the school grounds with flower beds, trees and brick paving.

The foyer is usually busy. The parent and toddler group meets here four mornings a week. Easy chairs are arranged at the back of the foyer behind a curved wall, so the group meets in the centre of the school, but is shielded from passing onlookers. There are 'Welcome' signs in all the children's languages. The notice boards have lists of groups and support services for parents, and details about local councillors and their surgeries. A large notice announces that Cleves is an inclusive school and that we welcome all local children as part of the Newham policy.

Brigid

> I have been a head teacher at another school, an early years educational home visitor, and an LEA inspector, so I came to Cleves with lots of ideas about what I wanted to do. I know some parents find it very difficult to come into school because of their own experiences of school as children. It is important to remember that many parents have had a negative first experience of education. Just to step through the doorway is a bit scary.

You have to enable them to do those first couple of steps in as comfortable a way as you can, by being welcoming and friendly so that they can go onwards from there. I think it is important that we are all called by first names here. I think some parents find that hard because they expect teachers to be distant and to tell them off. Sometimes they are angry and treat you badly at first, as if to test you. When we first opened, our approach was quite difficult for some parents, because they remembered sitting formally at a desk, and even if they had failed at school they wanted a similar experience for their children.

Some adult sports clubs use the school building and grounds, and a children's play scheme uses one wing during the summer holidays. The staff talk with individual parents in the parents' meeting room, where the women's support group, and the parents' support group for families with children with special needs, also meet. School governors and local councillors talk with parents here. The preschool home visiting team holds a weekly opportunity group for families with children with special needs in the early years wing. We have weekly keep fit sessions for staff and parents.

Jasweer

I work in all the schools in the borough and I work for a voluntary organisation, SPINN – Supporting Parents Inclusion Network Newham – to support parents whose children need special education. We meet at Cleves every week though some parents have children at other schools. We advertise all over the borough to all Asian parents. We discuss the children's education and special education. The parents support one another through discussions which are informal but confidential. Sometimes other issues come up, and I'm able to suggest they share these with another group; there is a domestic violence group on Wednesdays. Some parents might join us through a parent and toddler group.

I help them with filling in forms, choosing schools and if they meet with a language barrier. The borough's policy is that the best school for a child with special needs is the one nearest to the home (though some schools like Cleves have extra resources). The group has been going for three or four years, and on average six to ten parents attend. Cleves School is a good place to meet because it is very friendly and open with a nice building. It's accessible and the parents' room is good. It is not stuck away somewhere at the back of the school but is by the front door. We don't interrupt the smooth running of the school, and they let us make tea and coffee here. We work as a good team in SPINN, and the parents have all this open information.

Parents tend to agree with the staff that the school is a valued amenity. They comment, for example:

It's really friendly here. I re-started this parent and toddler group because we were sitting here talking, and we arranged with Brigid and Debbie (head and deputy head) to build it back up again. They were very helpful. We've got a free run of the foyer, all the toys are provided, the ball pool and things, we don't have to pay anything out, we just have to make sure

An inclusive community school

The carer and toddler group meets in the school foyer

we have money for the tea and coffee and biscuits and that's it. We make the tea in the kitchen here just off the foyer. So it's very cheap and that's a bonus. There's not a lot of organising to do. We get a few mothers from other schools here but it is mainly ones from Cleves. We drop our children off here at 9 o'clock and we stay on. I like to think we're a friendly group. There's quite a few other parent–toddler groups, but there's not a lot else to do round here. If I didn't come here, I'd be at home, bored. And here it's meeting other adults and getting rid of your problems. I don't think there are any other facilities for young families.

Other mornings when we don't have the parent–toddler group we sometimes sit around here, one day I didn't go home till twelve. I really do like it. It's like a second home. You don't have to wait outside for your kids, you can come in. I've got no problems here. I feel this school is different, more open and Brigid is very friendly. You can talk to her about anything and you know it will be all right.

The wings

The building branches into four wings, for early years with reception, and for Key Stages 1, and 2A and 2B. Each wing has up to 120 children and 12 staff. The layout of the wings supports the inclusive education methods. Each wing has a central activity room with four rooms leading off it. There are no doors between the five rooms and the children move around the whole wing during the day. Each room is used for different kinds of learning: two rooms, formerly separately for reading and writing, are now used for literacy, another for maths, one for finding out (science and humanities) and the central room is mainly for technology and creative work. The four side rooms are also the base rooms for up to 30 children and their base teacher.

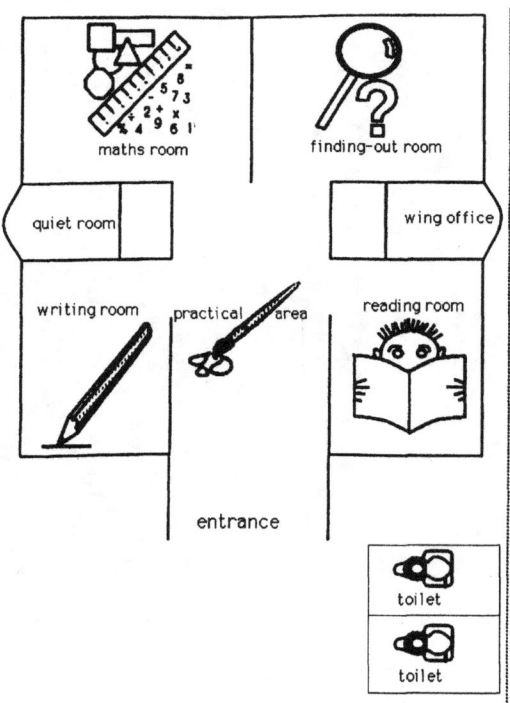

Key stage 2B wing

As you go into a wing, you enter the central practical room first, well lit by skylights. Some wings are brightly painted, one has orange-pink walls for instance. Visitors say it is rather like coming into a beehive where everyone is busy, all engaged in their own activities, individually or in small or large groups. Each wing has its own toilets and pegs for coats and bags, with store cupboards and two small rooms. These are used as staff offices, computer rooms, quiet areas and for small group learning. Some of the small rooms are decorated in the theme of a jungle or an ocean. All the rooms have carpets except the central one.

Furniture and movement

The learning areas do not have a chair and table space for every child. Instead, three pairs of small tables may be set out, or there may simply be low shelves and tables round the sides of the rooms to provide work spaces. A base room for up to 30 children might have only 12, 16 or 20 chairs, and these are often stacked away at one side.

This has several advantages. Instead of the furniture tending to control the children's movements and learning activities, there is plenty of space for everyone to move around, including children who use a rollator (walking frame with wheels) or a wheelchair. There is also ample space for the displays and equipment needed for all the subjects in the curriculum, such as science or art. Much equipment can be left ready for use in each wing, rather than

We can work at tables or on the floor

having to be especially set out and put away. The children can find and use almost everything they need in their own wing. They can quickly change their working space: from maths at a small table to pottery on a large one; from drama with a small group in a spacious spare corner, to reading on a small sofa, to a group discussion. And for this, they may sit on the carpet or quickly find a few chairs. They form and reform large or small groups easily because they are used to doing this, and do not identify with any particular space or chair or group.

Many people feel uncomfortable and restless if they sit in the same chair for most of the day. Outside school, children tend to move around, for example, while they do their homework. They might perch on a sofa, kneel at a coffee table, lean or stand against a worktop or rest on a cushion. Some children at Cleves cannot sit still for long, and inclusive education involves encouraging children to concentrate for as long as they can, by letting them move and change activities when they feel they have to. Many other children benefit from this flexibility. As Harsumeet comments:

> We can move around a lot. I like that and it's different from some other schools because you have to sit down still there most of the time. I need to move around, and when you know that you can, somehow it's easier to work, easier to concentrate. You don't keep looking at the clock to know when you can move.

Teacher's comment

> The children have more space to move around. The central hall is like a breathing space to them. It's nice for them and it's also nice for the teachers.

When space is used for activities rather than for furniture, this reduces the times when people knock against objects or against each other and start arguments. The wide range of equipment in each wing reduces the need for children to move to other parts of the school and for staff to supervise and escort them. A recent study found that 22 per cent of learning time may be used up in moving between activities in secondary schools (Griffith 1998). Moving the whole class tends to involve having to interrupt children who are absorbed in their work, and to make others wait until well after they are ready to go. This can undermine their concentration and interest, when periods are too long for some and too brief for others. It is then harder for teachers to control the class during learning sessions, and also between sessions when moving larger groups around the school, and waiting while they queue.

Like other schools (McNamara and Moreton 1995), we find that classes work more harmoniously, and children feel more liked and accepted by their peers and at ease with them, when they can all work together and know one another well. This is achieved through flexible grouping and regrouping, rather than when children strongly identify with only one or two subgroups in the class. At first, teachers may find that attempts to regroup a class which is not used to moving around can be so disruptive that they are discouraged from trying to work more flexibly. However, when children are used to organising their own groups they can do so easily, especially when there is enough space, and when carpets keep down the noise levels and are often used instead of chairs.

Members of Key Stage 2B describe their wing

In the central practical room, we've got equipment for lots of work – construction and puzzles, technology, modelling, science and music, art. There's old typewriters and new and old computers for technology, and a solar powered little aeroplane. We do all sorts of things every week. We often do painting and drawing, printing, mosaics and collages, textiles and sculpture. We can easily get out any activity. All the trays and the cupboard doors have pictures of the different equipment, as well as the names, so people who can't read words know where the things are kept too. And of course we can see where to put them away again. Everyone has to put things away when they have finished, and help tidy up twice a day. At the end of the summer term we have a big spring clean and clear out. On the walls there are our copies of pictures by Monet and Van Gogh. And we drew the front cover of a book of Greek myths, and there's a huge Minotaur which three people painted.

The wings have water trays and sand or clay set out. There is a big kiln in one of the side rooms, with shelves to dry our pottery. We have to do the clay work properly, with no bubbles left in to blow up and smash other people's things in the kiln. Over the shelves where we keep our own trays, there are worktops all round the central room. We do our diaries there (see later). At the tables in the middle, we can work in groups. As we've got cloakrooms and toilets in each wing, we can go to the toilet any time, we don't have to ask.

An inclusive community school

Then you go through these wide doorways into the other four main rooms. They're our home bases (class or registration groups), with about 30 children and our teacher. We meet in our home base when we come into school and at 11.30 until we go to lunch, and again at about 3.00 for the end of the day. We sit on the floor and we read poems and stories and talk, and do puzzles and games, all sorts of things.

Each home base is also a learning area. In the writing one, we are doing books about ourselves to take to secondary school, and we write about what sort of things we're going to miss. I'm going to miss the teachers and all the children and my friends. In our next school we'll all have to sit in class rooms at tables and not be able to move around, and we won't be able to choose the order we do our work in. In the writing room we've got displays of different scripts and alphabets, Gujarati, Punjabi and Tamil. We do different kinds of writing and our names are written in those scripts next to our work. A Japanese helper came in to show us how to do Japanese writing and we painted mountains and made fans and did origami.

In the finding-out room we done the Greeks, their maths, and we've made all different masks, vases, scrolls, shields, swords. And we had a Greek Olympics and the winning teams won medals we made. We all made tiles with pictures and patterns on, and some did Greek designs. They was very nice but we left them outside, and some men and children came, not from our school, and broke them and was on the roof destroying our school.

It's all right to walk through the rooms while everyone is working. The teachers don't mind, and we get lots of visitors. We can read sitting on the floor or on cushions or little sofas. We've got quiet areas behind the bookshelves. All the wings have rugs and cushions for the children with toys and mobiles and easy books.

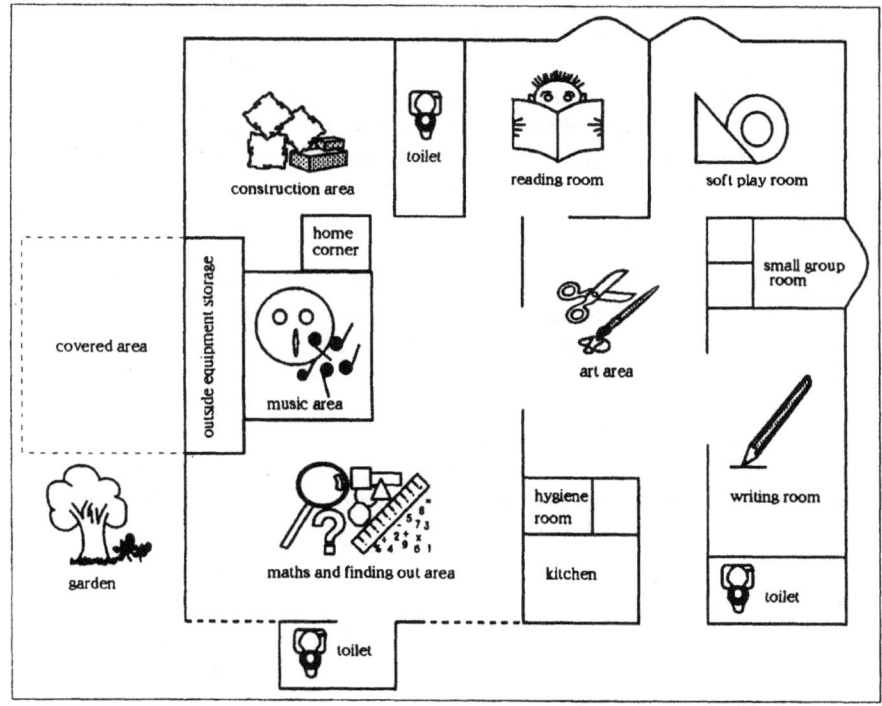

Early years wing

The early years garden is another classroom

Joy, early years team leader

The early years garden is used rather as an extra room. We have a big canopy in the playground. That is so important, those children in high rise flats desperately need to move, and run around and be free. We've always got a teacher out there on duty for an hour and a half each morning and afternoon. It's equipped as an outdoor classroom and the curriculum takes place outside there just as much as inside. It just needs staff who will use it fully. We take turns to work in each area for a week. But when it's cold weather, because we're team-spirited, we'll say to the teacher outside, come in and warm up, and she'll have a cup of tea and work in the maths and finding-out area for a while, before she goes out again. But we never don't go out just because of the weather, we think it's crucial. I feel the children need to be on their feet, running and moving. A lot of children can't move around much at home and then they go into cramped class rooms with desks. Some of our rooms are quite small, but you can spill out of them into the other rooms, and see loads of space all around. When the children all share the wing, they have much more equipment and much more space than if they were all inside their own class room.

The children's attendance is really good. It's sometimes quite hard to make them stay at home if they are sick. So I say to parents, 'We'll try it. Let them come and see how they get on and I'll let you know if they are really poorly.' They go up and down very quickly, and some recover once they start working and being with their friends. If children don't feel well, in all the wings we can lay out pillows and quilts in a quiet corner.

The staff

From the start, we wanted 'child-centred' staff who like having an inclusive approach through an integrated day, and having children moving around having conversations and discussions and not just chalk and talk. We set out those principles. Everyone was enthusiastic, although some of the staff found it easier to encourage group activities than others did, and we had really challenging discussions about flexible teaching methods and curriculum programmes.

The funding is for one base teacher for up to 30 pupils, plus a curriculum support teacher, and we used to have five teachers per wing of up to 120 children. There is also the dedicated budget for pupils with special needs which covers extra welfare and support staff. We became concerned about the rising ratio of relatively untrained staff, so the governors decided that we should have fewer untrained and support staff in total, but increase the expertise by having trained nursery nurses and six teachers in each wing. Now, each wing has four teachers with their base group of up to 30 children each, and a fifth teacher specialises in curriculum support – on expanding the teaching and learning methods and resources so that children of all abilities can work with the curriculum. The sixth teacher is the team leader.

Each wing also has about six learning support staff, who include nursery nurses and welfare assistants. Their work is mainly in curriculum support for children with special needs, although all the children work with all the staff in their wing. We wanted to get away from the idea that any child needs 'one-to-one' support. One reason is that this support can lead to a child being rather isolated from other children and staff. Our assistants work as links rather than barriers, to ensure that while the most disabled children have adequate support they also have plenty of opportunities to play and work with the other children and staff. We aim to provide curriculum support, rather than primarily physical or emotional care, for every child.

There is one mid-day assistant and she works in the early years wing where some of the morning children stay on, and some afternoon children arrive early, for lunch. All the staff do lunch time duty, including the head teacher who also does some teaching.

The staffing levels at Cleves work out at one teacher for every 18 children and one learning support assistant for every 18 children. This costs the same as staffing budgets in other local authorities. The difference is that Newham does not have very highly staffed special schools and relatively under-staffed mainstream schools. By bringing all the local children together, they can all benefit from higher staffing levels. There is the added benefit that the disabled children and the other children gain so much from each other.

The learning support team and other visitors

As an inclusive school we have help and information from regular visitors. Newham LEA's immensely helpful Learning Support Team includes members of the visual impairment service, the hearing impairment team, the general learning support team, and someone from the autistic continuum support. Like all other schools we have the educational psychologist and school nurse and doctor. From the Health Authority we have speech therapists, occupational therapists and physiotherapists. The speech and language therapists work with early years children, as well as one day a week for children with statements and another half day for children with difficulties but no statement. We also have a visiting drama teacher, and a member of the English Language Service worked on a Bangladeshi Achievement Project between home and school.

Team teaching

The 12 or 13 staff in each wing work as a team. Besides having their own base group of children, the four base teachers work with every child in the wing, spending two weeks in turn in the four main activity rooms: literacy, maths and finding out. The shared expertise of all the staff enables us to cover a very wide curriculum for children of all abilities. Dividing up the preparation and teaching time among the team means that each session can have more staff time and attention than if one teacher covered the whole curriculum separately for each base group. Each teacher doesn't have to be good at the whole curriculum, which can be hard in a primary school.

Jim, a team leader

> Team teaching is good when it all works well and people are getting on with each other, and know what they are doing and are managing to overcome the challenges. The logistics can be horrendous with so many children and so many staff, to try to keep an overview of it all in your head is a bit of a nightmare. Because it is such a wider, bigger picture, it gives you a lot more challenge. As a class teacher, if you get trapped in a room and you have got conflict with a child, it can be a very lonely job, and you have to deal with it day in day out. Here, there is much more adult interaction which is an absolute god-send at times because you can bounce off ideas and share problems. If one of us has discipline problems with a child, we can very easily pass them on to some one else, and it is like a clean slate. There's no aggression, but that can build up in the class room. I haven't had to spend much time on sorting out differences between the adults. It definitely helps that this is a very supportive system to work in. We are with each other all the time, and a lot of 'bonding' goes on.

Joy, early years team leader

> I think when you are in a team of people, there's an element of wanting to do well because you don't want to let the others down. And, just to stimulate yourself, we do get nearly all the equipment out everyday, so it's all used as far as possible. Some of the resources can be simple things, like making sure we've got sensory equipment like jam or cornflakes or pasta twirls. They don't cost a fortune but somebody has to go to Tesco's after school to stock up, somebody has to be committed. Our SENCO is very good giving us ideas and practical help.

Mary, a base teacher

I think the authority here is different, it is more implicit. I had a bad experience as a class teacher and I was going to leave teaching. I am still trying to work out how Cleves is very different. It values the individual and is so person-centred and that gets rid of the power, no one's got to play a power game because you are accepted for who you are and for what gifts you have to offer. This goes from teacher to pupil, you are empowering each other. I think that's why the team is very strong because you can draw on people's different gifts, and that raises self-esteem. When Brigid wants something done, she approaches you and talks about it often in a way that makes you want to do it. If people try to play the power game here it just doesn't work; they either leave because they can't cope and they want that class room back for themselves, or they change.

Lyn, teacher responsible for computers and information technology (IT)

Teachers soon realise whether they like working with team work. They have to get on well with one another, and communication is so important. In any team of staff there will always be some difference but we hope that most of the time we can sort it out in an amicable way. We have weekly team meetings when we plan the next week. If someone wants to do something the others don't agree with, or if someone is becoming too dominating, it is talked through. There will always be some differences and complaints but we would hope that they are brought out in the open. If someone dominates then it becomes very hard work, but people realise when they come to work here that you have to compromise, because this system is so team-orientated, and talking about work is also socialising. We usually sit and chat for a while after school. We have team meetings one night a week and whole staff meetings one night a week, until about 5.30. Senior management meet on another day a week. With traditional teaching, teachers can become very isolated, just you and the children all day, whereas here you are communicating and working with other adults all day, and there is a sense of community at the wing level in the open plan approach to learning.

Another teacher's comments

As teachers, we don't have our own classrooms. We move round the curriculum areas. So for two weeks we teach reading and for two weeks maths, and so on. It is not at all boring because you are moving on all the time, moving children through. It is a good way of helping them to progress, by staying with them. We used to just do it for a week, and we found that quite often we weren't getting to all the children and that it's better when we have a two-week period. Probably if you were only working with a small group of children, like 30, it wouldn't be so interesting, but here we work with about 120 and it's great.

One advantage of the high staffing levels and the team teaching is that they relieve stress among staff, and this is shown by the lower sick leave absences. When staff attend courses, colleagues can cover for them. We therefore have less need to employ supply staff, and everyone's work can be more consistent, with greater continuity in teaching and support. The team teaching also allows more time off for training. With the recent introduction of the literacy hour, for example, one teacher from each wing has been able to spend days on training and also on helping other staff in the wing. Team teaching can support new and supply teachers, as some of them commented:

> So far, I like team teaching, the equal sharing of ideas, the fairness of the equality. It is easier to settle into the school when you're working with a team instead of independently in your own classroom. It's more enjoyable to work with other adults, to talk about plans and bounce around ideas, whereas I found it rather boring to plan sessions on my own. Just by sitting and talking with two or three other people for 30 or 40 minutes after school, you get so many more ideas and you come up with better ones. Certain people might have expertise in certain subjects and they'll say they'd like to do that, or they'll give you ideas about how to do it. They seem very creative here.
>
> The weekly planning meeting is mainly about finding out what is going on in each area, rather than saying 'You've got to do this'. We have termly and half-termly plans. The meeting will cover what we have been doing in each area and how that work can be developed and what can be put into the plans. One current topic is patterns within nature but we can decide whether to do bark or shell patterns – bouncing off ideas in a team, and with such a diverse range of people working here, there are always new ideas about what we could do. The support staff share in some of the teachers' meetings to discuss sessions or certain children and they also have their own meetings. We talk about the activities we will all set out each morning and how we can, say, make the learning more tactile. The support staff will suggest activities they could set out alongside the mainstream planning and connected with the targets, and all the children can use those if they wish, it's not a question of a child with needs working alone.

The pace with the team teaching is fast and intense, and it is important that someone, the team leader, and also the head and deputy head, hold the anxiety. It is very demanding, dealing with 120 children, knowing them all well, and being able to track what they do and know what help they need, with the different ways of relating to different children, and issues that are raised by parents when they come in.

Team teaching can be more inclusive, because in enclosed classrooms there may be only one child with special needs. Yet here, no one child is isolated, there are always other children like them. It is the same with being the only black child or the only girl. When they are in separate classes, support staff may draw out the special needs children for group work. That is fine if everyone goes out in groups, but not if only some children do.

In order to ensure that team teaching works well, detailed records are kept and shared by the staff. Each wing has a new booklet each year on wing management and on the curriculum plans, as well as using the curriculum plans for each subject produced for the whole school. The teams in each wing plan the curriculum details. The curriculum is driven interdependently by

- the needs of the children, as detailed in their previous records,
- the development of skills, concepts, attitudes and knowledge, that are necessary for effective learning, and
- the content of the National Curriculum and RE.

All plans are constantly reviewed and refined through ongoing observation and assessment. The value of differentiated teaching and learning is that all children, from those with learning difficulties to the most able, are encouraged to work towards their own best possible level, even when they are working on the same overall topic.

The National Curriculum Programme of Study is organised into six termly plans for each wing, three for each year group. They provide the core and foundation subjects which staff then organise into termly foci. Detailed plans for each subject also take account of cross-curricular themes. The subjects are planned termly under the headings of:

- aims
- concepts, skills, attitudes and knowledge
- National Curriculum reference
- objectives (examples of activities), including IT and cross-curricular links
- resources required
- assessment.

So, for example, the termly maths sheet will have spaces for each of these headings to be used.

The final details are planned by the staff who decide their work rotas, of two weeks in turn in the five learning areas. Each area has access to information technology. Information from the termly planners is outlined on half-termly overview sheets, stored along with weekly and daily planning sheets in a file in each curriculum area. The weekly year-group sheets give details under the following headings (using the example of the maths sheet):

- focus
- recording methods
- learning outcomes 1, 2, 3
- groups (of children concerned) with the differentiated resources required and assessment methods.

Each child's own weekly maths sheet has these headings:

- ongoing learning opportunities,

1. using and applying
2. number and algebra
3. shape, space and measurements
4. handling data

with lists of planned activities under each item,

- learning outcomes 1, 2 and 3
- evaluation and opportunities for continuation

and work produced with examples kept with the record so that staff can easily review them.

Home–school links

Parents are very helpful with activities in the school and with school trips, and there are active parent governors. When parents come to help in the wings, some read stories in community languages. Benin in Nigeria was on the National Curriculum, so one of our governors, a grandmother who was a headmistress in Nigeria for 30 years, came in to teach that. We welcome people with specialist skills – musicians, artists, industrialists, actors and footballers. We aim to work closely with the parents.

Debbie

In early years teaching, there is a big focus on working with parents. That lays the foundations and it is very important then, because you tend to see parents less, as the child gets older. Often, until they come here, those parents have been the only carer for their child. It takes a lot of reassurance for them to be able to hand over their child. We encourage parents to stay as long as they want, to settle their child in, and as long as their child needs them and they feel comfortable. Sometimes we say, 'We'll go and sit outside for ten minutes and have a coffee, then come back and see how well she can get on if you're not there.' They are often anxious and need someone to talk to.

Once children with needs are identified, I do home visits before the children start school and I am the liaison person for parents to contact. They start here at three years and quite a few of our children come to our mixed opportunity group on Wednesdays, from about 18 months of age. We work with the education office and preschool home visiting team, to try to identify children as early as possible so they can come to school when they are three.

They could come full-time, but we try to make it as normal as possible. Children usually attend half of every day at first and build up to a full-time place. Non-disabled children may be in much greater need of a full-time place, perhaps because of their home circumstances, so we look at the whole range of needs and try to identify the children who would most benefit from an early full-time place. Children with needs usually stay for lunch after the morning, or they come for lunch before their afternoon sessions.

Joy

Because it's such an open school, the parents can come in and get help from each other and there's a strong parents' network. Or they might ask for help from a nursery nurse rather than a teacher, because of their own experiences at school, things were different then. Or they might ask a childminder, if they want to ask about handling difficulties. One of the staff meets every child at home before they start to attend to help them to settle in. We encourage parents to stay and to help because of the benefits this brings for the school.

If we are concerned about a child we have a team meeting. If we think there may be some violence, we involve Brigid, because she's the named person for child protection, and we discuss any worries with her. Then we work on a strategy – whether to contact social services, or the parent directly, or work with the child and outwards that way. The team approach here at Cleves is much stronger and more effective than anywhere else I have worked. We never work in isolation. We must always preserve the relationship with the parent, and the parents' dignity, because we've got to move forward with that child, hopefully for quite a number of years.

We try to be really flexible, and helpful and approachable. We often do help out, where there might be, let's say, some kind of aggression happening. We're able to relieve it, act as a safety valve. And they know, I think, that we're very understanding and not judging. Sometimes there might be social workers involved, and we try to liaise, and get them through their problems, talk about handling children, invite them in to watch how the staff handle them and set boundaries and guidelines and deal with children without smacking them, because people think that's the way to do it, and maybe for them it is. But if we can show them there are other ways to set the boundaries, it's quite helpful for them – to pick up our language, and sit and watch what we do. And they tell us, usually, later on that it has been successful, it has worked. We move forward as a team. We can also tell them so many positives: 'Oh yes! They counted today. They did their beads. They read a word.' So we're always giving them lots of good things.

With the children with special needs we write their home–school books every afternoon – what they've done during the day, and achieved, whether they managed to use the toilet. We're relating to the kinds of things parents would notice at home, so there's some kind of rapport going on. Learning doesn't just happen here at school, it happens at home. So we pick up on things, and ask how their families are. The children bring their pets in, and photographs of their holidays to Pakistan, for example. We see the holidays as an important mark in their life when they learn a lot.

I think we all know how important it is to be empathic with the parents and have close ties between the home and school. And we don't have uniforms or use surnames. These things are barriers and we try our best to knock all those down.

Brigid

We work closely with the parents, we have termly reports and parents' meetings. Something like 50 to 55 per cent of parents turn up, which is very good. The children come too, and staff in the wings set up activities for them to do. The staff chat to the parents in a more private place, and the children can join in if they want to.

At every termly review for children with special needs, we start off by asking the parents first for their views, and then the teachers and other staff will give their views afterwards. The reviews are half-termly when the child starts here or, if there are any changes, we might have an informal meeting to talk about it. If the parents need to discuss their child with a doctor, either the curriculum support teacher, or someone on the staff who speaks their language, might go with them. But you have to get a balance between nurturing and enabling. Part of our role is to empower parents to demand their rights.

Getting the balance partly depends on the family. If we feel the family can manage to organise and get to their appointments we'll leave them to do that. If we feel they need our support to do the first or the second we'll do that, or help them later on. For example, today Debbie is going with one mother to the housing department for the first appointment, but after that we will leave her to organise things, though we'll probably ring her up and ask how things are going. Ultimately she'll have to make decisions and choices for herself, and our role, as with the children, is to help them to be able to do this too.

A parent's comment

I find they [school staff] are very much in tune with the mothers. If the mothers have problems, they're very willing to assist. If I had a problem, I wouldn't feel at all embarrassed to come and talk to them about it. I'm married, I've got a good home, my husband's got a good job, but I'm still asking them to take my youngest one in as soon as possible because he needs it, and I find him hard to cope with. The most I do with my son, if I'm not at home, is to bring him here to the early years wing. There's a soft play room or the toddler group. There's nowhere else to go, and at home he never stops, he's up and down stairs, in the cupboards. I'm not made to feel that I'm treated perhaps with less empathy, because my circumstances are okay. They'll give as much care or listen to my problems as they would with a mother with six kids left on her own in a small flat. I feel that if they liked any parent more, they would never reveal that and that's what I call professional, and that's how it should be, because obviously everybody has their own opinions. I like the fact that everybody feels at ease.

Individual curriculum plans (ICPs)

Every child has an ICP for two reasons. One is to inform parents about the National Curriculum so they can understand and support their child's school work. The other reason is that the children with special needs tend to have detailed reports which are like ICPs, and we believe that all the children should be treated the same way. So we came to a decision, eventually, to have ICPs, which was quite hotly debated because of the amount of work it takes. We have never had a problem about staff not doing what has been agreed. We work together with democratic methods. People have two days off to write the aims of the ICPs for each child, and to write up the achievements. The aims are agreed first at team meetings.

As shown, when teachers take over a new activity area each fortnight, they check each child's written records and, if necessary, also check with the previous teacher. Most staff are already familiar with all the children in the wing through their contact with them in other activity areas during the previous six weeks, and their contact in the same activity area six weeks earlier. The children stay in each wing for two years. Regular formal and informal staff discussions also help to ensure the teachers' continuing knowledge of the children, with a emphasis on appreciating their achievements, and trying to understand reasons and possible solutions for any problems they may have.

The base teachers have overall responsibility for completing the records of the children in their base. Team teaching makes it easy for them to consult other staff when making these records, and they use the detailed weekly records that are continually kept about each child's main activities. In the ICPs at the beginning of each term they complete the aims and record of needs for each child, informed by previous achievements and National Curriculum requirements. Teachers also complete the child's records, assessed against the aims, before the end of term. Assessment takes many forms, such as observing, questioning, and seeing how the child applies knowledge in a specific task.

There is an observation file in each learning area, and detailed achievements are recorded there of activities and groupings to inform future planning, teaching and staff discussions. Samples of the children's work every term in all subjects, with annotations, are stored as part of a celebration of the child's achievements. These are shared at the termly (for some children half-termly) meetings with the parents. The termly reports with additional information contribute to each child's annual report in July.

Brigid

I read all the ICPs, or the senior management team does. I try to read them from the point of view of the parents – will they understand them, what will they want to know, like about their child's maths, are they motivated? If there are any gaps or some ambiguity, I send them back. Generally people are very good at doing them. From September they will be computerised with a dictionary of comments and aims. The backs of the ICPs have spaces for parents and the child to comment if they want to. For example, a boy said he would like to be better at spelling and maths and music, and he wrote 'I did my best at my SATs and I worked hard' and that is true.

Kim

As chair of the governors, I really believe in the ethos – it was that which drew me to the school. I live locally. When I first looked round the school, I thought the children seem to mix in well. The staff were friendly, they did not seem to be intimidated by the governors, and they totally believe in inclusive education.

As a child I went to a special boarding school, where I had a very good education and the staff were very committed. But I think I would have formed better relationships in the community if I had not been at a special

A governor's view

school, and some of the pupils there lost a great deal, they grew away from their families and became institutionalised, as if their whole world revolved around school. I was a boarder but I was lucky to have a close family. At that time, the local authorities assumed you would stay at school all term, and it wasn't until the end of my time there that they began to arrange transport for us to go home at weekends. Before that, parents had to arrange the transport and to make quite an effort if we were to be able to go home at weekends during term time. The thinking then was very much if you have a disability then you need to be sent away to a special school.

I can't say categorically that I would have had such a good education if I had been in a mainstream school, but I would at least liked to have had the opportunity to try it. The systems are much better now, and children with special needs in mainstream classes are picked up if they are not reaching their milestones, and given extra help. As the link governor for special educational needs, I'm responsible to see that any shortcomings or any lack of equipment or gaps are followed up.

I come into the school twice a term, and usually for other meetings too, to talk to the SENCO, and the staff, and for the governors' annual meeting with parents. We set up a system so that parents can contact me through the school, though they talk to the staff first and then only come to me if the problem cannot be resolved. I try to make sure I'm approachable. I have been on interview panels for appointing senior staff. I get my information for meetings in Braille. I find all the governors here are committed to inclusive education – they know before they start that's the school ethos.

The following chapters will show more about our links between the school and community, the staff and the families, between the staff teams and within the community of each wing.

Chapter 3
Active learning

This chapter describes the flexible learning day which is organised through the use of diaries. The main teaching approach is differentiated learning, in which groups of children at different ability levels work together on the same topics, each learning as much as they can in their own ways. The staff plan for differentiation both of task (the activities and resources the children work with) and of learning outcome. The aim is that people accept that they achieve different levels and everyone tries to do their own best. The curriculum must be challenging and based on high expectations of everyone in the school, building on their skills and achievements.

This chapter considers different learning styles, and the advantages which inclusive education can bring to all children. Inclusive methods with children with special needs are considered, and the complications of using standard assessments in all schools. Finally, we review the aims of our independent learning approach.

The flexible day and the diaries

The children share in planning their own day and moving between activities. This is an important part of inclusive education because, as we have mentioned, some of our children find it hard to stay still for long, but they take part in many activities through the school day when the timing can be adapted to each child's needs.

Doors around the single storey building lead from the school grounds straight into the wings. Before 9.00, children can choose individually whether to play outside or come into their wing. All the doors are locked from the inside so that staff and children inside open the doors for any child who wants to enter. This system ensures safety in several ways. The locks prevent strangers from entering the school unnoticed. Also, the children's easy access prevents the need for lining up, queues and mass movements though narrow spaces with the risks of being crushed or knocked over. Disabled children do not have the problem of trying to move quickly enough to keep in line. This kind of access, with children entering the building individually and in small groups, also prevents bullying and arguments, which tend to occur most frequently during lining up and crowded movements. Originally, we worked out how to avoid queues and crowds to protect the disabled children, and then we found that everyone benefited and opportunities for poor behaviour were greatly reduced. The children move around sensibly, like the adults. The day begins peacefully as the children come in between 8.45 a.m. and 9.00 a.m. and start to fill in their diaries. The teachers welcome the children individually and mark the dinner register. Then everyone sits together on the carpet to talk about the coming day. Delicia describes how we plan the day. This was the term before the literacy hour began, which is described later.

Delicia

> We do diaries, and I like that. You put your name on the cover and you have ten sheets for ten days. When you come in the morning you fill in your diary. Each day you write the date, then you have to do your targets: reading, writing, maths and finding out. You put the numbers next to them, in the order you want to do them. You choose your own order. Sometimes you might do maths all morning because it's interesting and you want to get on with it. So the next day you have to do other things first, and leave maths till last. If lots of people all want to start with maths or with reading and the room is very crowded then some of us have to go and do our next target first.

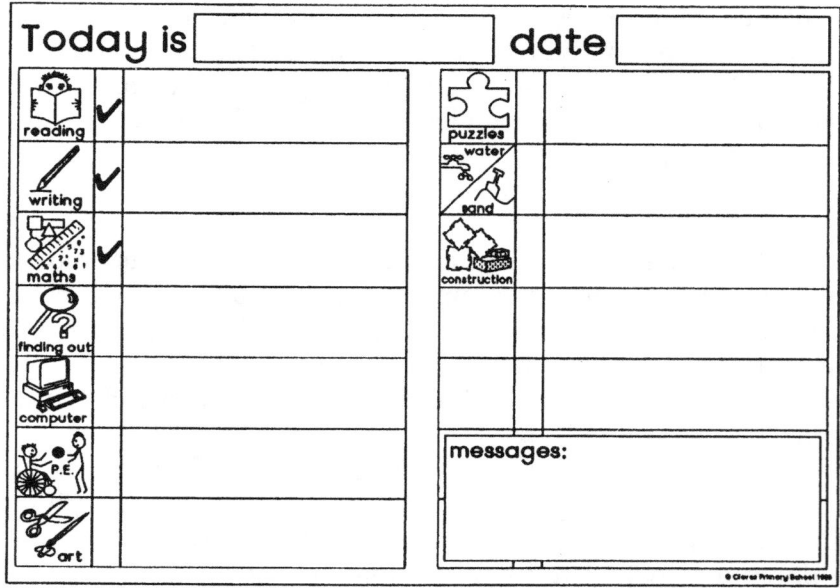

Key Stage 1 organisation and management. Each daily page in the diary has space for planning on one side of the page and evaluation on the other.

We take turns in having a go. We can go on the computer for 40 minutes and then stop so other people can have a turn and we mustn't moan because we've had our turn, but it's very upsetting when you can't finish your work. The next day you can go on it again, and every day until you've finished your work. You can carry on for a long time if no one else wants to use it. If we don't know what to do and we're waiting for the teacher to tell us, then we can come and do other things while we're waiting. Say we done reading and writing all the morning and afternoon one day, then we have to plan maths and science first the next day and plan reading and writing last. Those are our four targets, and when we've done them, we can do other things later.

Michael

When you've finished your target you write next to it what you've done, and what you think about it, and you write down what your teacher thinks about your work. We check with the teacher before we move on. Then the teacher gives a little sign and a tick. The teachers don't write their records in your diary, they write them in their record books. And if you've worked very hard you go to Brigid and get jewelled cats (stickers). In Key Stage 1, they colour in their diary in the box next to each target what they think about their work. Red means I liked it, blue means I didn't like it or I didn't do it very well, and yellow means somewhere in the middle. We have prizes for the best-kept diary.

Sanjeed

When I write my evaluations I'll say: 'I sketched a butterfly and coloured it in'. And I might write 'it was good' or 'it was excellent'. I try to get it good before I finish. Johnnie [teacher] said to us you have to do it for at least an hour to get it good. If it's good you might get 'JC' on it and you can go and get a jewelled cat. Everyone likes getting those.

The diaries help to ensure that everyone has worked to a reasonable level or extent before moving on to the next activity. The younger ones colour in, and the older ones write evaluations. For example:

> In finding out I drew a picture of a panda but it took a long time.
> I did painting with two colours.
> In finding out, I finished my model off.
> In PE I did free choice inside and it was fun. I worked with Amy and Sasha.
> In literacy I did some alphabetical orders and I liked that.
> I played basketball and I won and I got a jewelled cat.

Notes on the wall suggest phrases to use in the diaries:

> I planned, I learned, I found out, I researched, I worked hard to . . .
> The teacher may sign a space, or write a comment: such as 'Joanne worked on final letter sounds rhyming words. She worked very hard all afternoon.'

Active learning

The children are generally enthusiastic, as one supply teacher commented:

> I really like the open plan system, it's easier for supply teachers. I find the children do benefit from the freedom of choice to plan their day. They are certainly confident about planning and evaluating their work. They soon find what their strengths are, and you might expect them to opt for those activities and the practical ones, but they don't. They're very keen to do maths and literacy and they're aware of the need to do different activities at different times of the day. I find that my base group tend to do academic subjects first in the day. They want to learn, and they like the structure of the literacy hour compared with the greater freedom for the rest of the day.

Lyn, IT teacher

I don't know if the organisation goes a long way towards motivating the children, or whether it is the careful preparation we do, or the freedom they have, planning their own day instead of being teacher-directed all the time. For example, if the children don't feel like doing PE first thing in the morning, they can do it in the afternoon if they like, there are four slots during the day when children from our wing can go to PE.

Some children can't cope with this freedom, and some children take advantage of it as well. But part of our job as teachers is to identify them and make sure they are always on-task. We certainly don't have to do as much chivvying here. You notice at the beginning of the year when you have new children, that it takes them time to settle in and learn the expectations of what the work is about, to concentrate longer and do more focused activities each day.

I think if the children have some control over what they are doing, they are more enthusiastic. But we still have to control some of their activity. They might come in to do maths and just do a puzzle and say 'I've done my maths work'. And you have to say, 'But that's only part of it, you have to do some work with the teacher now.' So it is broadening out their horizons in that respect as well.

It can be difficult to regulate the flow of children. Like the last couple of weeks we've had the Roamer, a computerised robot that moves around the floor. Because it only comes out occasionally when we do specific work with it, everybody wants to use it at the same time. So we have a system that they write their names on a list, and when their name comes up they are called to do that work. That works OK and they understand about taking turns and having a fair chance at it.

We do occasionally group the children at the same level so that we teach them as a group, but not a huge group, maybe about six at a time. You would have to see the whole school to understand how we work. It is hard to explain, but I don't think there is ever a large group of children, 24–30 that is, working at the same level. [Except that the next term after Lyn made these comments, the literacy hour was introduced and this involves sessions with groups of up to 30. Assemblies and PE involve large groups but not the rest of the curriculum teaching.] This way we can teach across a wide range more equally and appropriately. It is definitely a more interactive way of teaching, and the children are far more independent here. They can come in and get on with things without teachers having to say constantly, 'Look, get on with this now. No, don't do that, come and do this now. This is finished, you have done it twice, that is enough.' They know when they have reached their limit, and they go on to do something else. There is a lot less lining up to have things marked and hands up waiting for help, a lot less time wasted.

Joy, early years leader

Some children play with one activity for a long time. It depends what it is. If I can justify that it involves some maths, a lot of language, cooperation, social skills, creativity, self-worth, all those things, then I'll happily let that go on. It's only if it gets not so interesting or a little bit negative that I'll urge them on to the next activity. We give them a badge when they finish maths, reading, writing and finding out. They are very proud of wearing the badges to show what they have achieved each day. I think instant gratification does work. We use the diary symbols and discuss them so that they are ready to use their diaries in Key Stage 1.

Logistics

Sometimes children choose tasks that are too easy. When this happens, the teacher checks that they also complete a harder, more appropriate, task before signing their diary and letting them move on. If this happens quite often, the teacher will talk to the child about why this might be happening, and take a more active part in helping the child to choose activities. While the early years children move fairly freely from task to task, as they become older, most children are expected to spend longer on each task, and for some activities to begin with group instruction before starting their own tasks. The children with a very short attention span are closely helped and supervised by the support staff. When children want to work with a friend or in a group on an activity that is too easy or hard, or too much in demand by several others, the staff may ask them to move to another area. Because the children know that they can usually negotiate and have a choice, that moving around is an integral part of the day not a punishment, and that if they are keen to do something they will probably be able to later in the day, they cooperate in forming and reforming groups, and in arranging with the staff and with each other how they do this.

A typical day with Key Stage 2A

We choose the order for our work and copy into our diaries the tasks listed that day on the white board. For example:

Reading:	literacy hour 10.15 a.m. – 11.15 a.m.
Writing:	literacy with Steve
Maths:	measuring, using centimetres and metres
Finding out:	light signals
	a surprise project
Painting:	patterns and symmetry
PE	park 1.30 p.m.
Dinner	12.00 noon
Wing assembly	11.30 a.m.

At 9.15 a.m. everyone goes to their first session. So many people go to maths first that Jim, the teacher, says, 'I've got too many friends and [names of two other teachers] are lonely. Who is going to see them now?' When enough people have left, the rest sit on the carpet near Jim and talk about metres. A learning assistant does physiotherapy with one boy nearby. The maths room wall displays have posters about the Islamic calendar and Ramadan prayer times. Later we move into small groups to work on shapes. Some people make a list of 30 objects in the room by their shape, some do work sheets, and others cut out printed sheets to make paper models of cubes and pyramids.

In the central activities room a girl and boy work at the sand tray and 14 boys and girls work in three groups drawing butterflies on squared paper for symmetry. A boy in a wheelchair uses stickle bricks and a lego zoo for a while. A group that has been looking at lights and prisms in a dark room walk through to the finding-out room where they write notes about what they have seen. Groups of three children each work at the three computers; one group is looking at a CD Rom about the body.

In the reading and writing rooms for two hours every morning, two groups of children do the literacy hour, 60 children in turn, while the other 60 children use the other three rooms. At about 11.40 a.m. everyone tidies up their room and then we all move into

Going up on the climbing frame in a wheelchair

one room for the wing assembly. We sit together on the carpet, and Jim, the team leader, praises us for working hard. Then each of the six teachers in turn says a little about the work which everyone in their area has been doing, and some hold up examples of good work. Jim then reads some funny poems and a story. After that, we begin to go through the doors leading straight into the playground where we play until we are called in small groups to the dining room.

During the afternoon, we all go to play in the park for PE. Later, in the finding-out room, some people work on lights and signals. One boy makes an electric eel with a torch to light up inside the head. He prefers to work on his own and to work out how to explain and write up what he is doing and why. Another listens to a musical toy. Some girls have drawn a juggling clown design on cardboard, each ball is going to be a small light bulb which will flash in turn. They read the instructions and test how to fit the wires so that they work correctly. They tape the wires onto the back of the cardboard and they share out different tasks to suit their friends with different abilities. One group is making a game with buzzers linking capital cities to countries.

Another group, working on an electricity experiment, is filling in a work sheet with these headings, that show how assessment is closely combined with learning and is often done by the children as well as the staff.

> What we are trying to find out:
> What I think will happen:
> Because:
> The equipment and materials we need:
> How we will make the test fail:
> What we will keep the same:
> What we will change:
> What we will observe/measure:

At the end of the day we tidy up and sit in our base groups to read a story before going home.

Shared activities

Work is often done in pairs and groups. Obviously, reading and writing are among the most vital skills to learn at school, and much of the day is spent on them. Yet most children read and write at well below the level of their thinking and their ability to talk about ideas. Through discussing ideas together they can clarify and expand one another's thinking, work at a deeper level of discovery and, through helping each other to understand, make their own breakthroughs to clearer understanding (McNamara and Moreton 1997). Although some teachers like their class to be quiet, it doesn't necessarily mean that they are working. Talking is an important way of learning, and of helping each other to learn through sharing ideas and discussing them. When talking is valued, and the children are used to working hard in small groups without needing adults to keep reminding them to concentrate, it can be quite noisy. But the teachers need not feel stressed or feel that noise means they are losing control. One teacher commented:

> I find some children [with communication difficulties] are quite vocal and they might drown out the voices of another child and it is a matter of finding out ways round that. Partly, I think, we all get used to some level of noise here. I can switch off from it completely and the children are used to the noise, they switch off and focus on their work and on what the teacher is explaining to them. They are very tolerant. I think it is important to learn to be able to concentrate while there is noise and activity around you. In an open plan area you are bound to have some noise.

Examples

- During the literacy hour, Paul and Hameed wrote a story together. The story had to be about a spaceship and had to use adjectives. They worked out the plot and the characters and each wrote out their copy, then they read it to the group saying alternate sentences. The story was about two boys who became friends and set out on a space adventure.
- Other joint activities include making pictures and models together, dividing a story of a cartoon strip into six parts with each person creating one part. There is paired reading. When doing experiments with batteries and light bulbs, many children work in pairs and small groups, all doing something different on a range of activities
- People usually use the computers in twos and threes rather than on their own, talking about their work together and taking turns. More children are then able to have a turn with the computers.
- With fractions, some children will go on to quite abstract discussion and written work but others will share out a cake. Everyone is included in that notion of learning about fractions with slightly different ways of doing it and all working together. Measuring millimetres, centimetres and metres, for instance, can be done by small groups.
- PE and games and the soft play area can all be shared activities and we often do parachute games and trust games. The children are very cooperative and collaborative. Staff set up the activities so that all the children can take part, and they help and support each other. You see rollators by the door, but you cannot tell which children on the PE apparatus use them because almost everyone is so actively involved.
- One group chose poems on racism and they devised a percussion backing track to go with the poetry readings. Making music easily involves children with a range of abilities and we do all kinds of music, from classical to pop.

During a science experiment, children can take part through differentiated tasks with differentiated outcomes as well. For instance, instead of asking someone to design a windsock, the teacher might ask children to look at ways they could measure the wind, setting an open-ended task. Some children might throw up powder paint in the air and see the wind carry it along, and some would make quite sophisticated mechanical ways of measuring, for example, things that whirl around.

We aim for these kinds of activities every day, so that everyone can be helpful and enabling to one another and also get their entitlement to the curriculum. New children in the school learn to do the same by watching and doing the same as the others. Every activity is of equal worth; sensory learning such as painting or learning with water can be as important as skilled reading or writing.

Varied activities

The National Curriculum ensures that all children learn a very wide range of topics each term. At Cleves, with all the staff working with all the children in their wing, we can draw on many kinds of expertise. The staff can thoroughly prepare, teach and assess their topics, working with individuals and small interactive groups.

During the spring term 1998, Key Stage 2B worked on activities including:

- learning about temperature and insulation, gases, liquids and solids;
- investigating land use and the water cycle;
- reading *Romeo and Juliet*, acting parts of it, and working on how emotions are felt physically;
- composing and recording music and using the pentatonic scale, drones and ostinato;
- copying the style of artists like Lowry;
- using the Internet and e-mail, including looking up artists on the Internet;
- talking about death and grief and Easter and writing poems about that;
- creating news reports on audio and video tapes;
- making advertising videos;
- learning about food packaging and advertising;
- writing a newspaper;
- working on the style and content of pamphlets;
- playing trust games which rely on team work to succeed (like the blindfold walk);
- hockey, netball, tennis and rugby;
- map and compass work, orienteering and hiking;
- learning about support agencies, Samaritans and Childline and the people who use them;
- talking about forgiveness and affirmation, truth and honesty;
- dancing to African and Asian music;

- thinking about moving on to secondary school and what it feels like to be new;
- gardening and creating a pond;
- spending a week on a barge in Essex.

Learning styles and assessment

Brigid

Whether or not you have a statement, your learning style may not be the same as other people's in your cohort. Therefore, we think schools should be organised around learning styles and paces. I'm an experiential learner. When I start at a computer I need to play about with it, other people may read the handbook. There's intuitive, there's visual, experiential, abstract learning, and people who use a mixture of all of these, and many more ways of learning. The role of schools is to enable you to be successful, and to look at different ways of enabling yourself to be successful.

The national climate tends increasingly to be about 'all people should learn the same way, with the same content and therefore the same outcome' – for admirable reasons. But it is about uniformity, and inclusion is about diversity because that is what the world is about. It is a real tension. Schools ought to be celebrated for their difference, and not have difficulties because they are different, as long as they can justify it.

Reading, writing and maths are a basic entitlement. We are failing children if we do not help them to learn these. But we have to question when is the best time to learn them. Is it when you are a particular age, or you are motivated to, or able to, or want to? There are many aspects to learning. It is not simply that if you give children a particular thing they will learn it.

Testing is an important part of education, and of knowing where someone stands within a set of things that they have been prescribed to learn. But tests are only one way of celebrating achievement, and there are many other ways. We celebrate that a child comes to school, the relationships they have, the tremendous amount of learning some of our children achieve during only two terms, which is not reflected in the National Curriculum tests results. The curriculum and ways of learning are different when you are seven or twelve years old. You may do very well at seven, but that does not necessarily mean you will do well at twelve when the learning is more abstract. Having bald figures to celebrate success is only a quarter of the story.

Some of our work will not show until much later on. In a way we are educating these children's children now, in the sense of negotiation instead of violence, seeing adults as supportive, being self-motivated and industrious in your own way, and the notion that you can learn in any circumstances, whatever happens to you, and that learning is a wonderful thing. There are also study skills, discussion, research, and investigative skills which are useful not just at school but for life. We hope that, at secondary school, our children will be much more skilled at dealing with a variety of people and circumstances, at finding out where they should be and what they should be doing, and at independent learning, questioning and listening and showing initiatives. Sometimes at secondary school you may not feel very confident about coming forward and saying 'Actually I was in the school play and I was quite good at it and I'd really like to do this.' Our staff keep saying 'Oh yes, that was really great, you ought to carry on doing this.' We say to them 'We expect you to go on to college or on to university.' This is helping a community to broaden out and understand that there are choices.

The literacy hour

Before introducing the literacy hour, we were concerned that it would make the day and the teaching methods less flexible and responsive to each child's needs. After a few weeks of having the literacy hour at the time of writing this book, it is too early to judge the real effects. We will assess them after a proper trial period, and if necessary adapt them, taking the good parts, changing parts and making them our own. However, we have found that several of our main inclusive, differentiated learning methods combine well with the literacy hour.

Newham LEA publish a teaching guide about the literacy hour. It shows how to use differentiated teaching methods which can help children of all abilities to gain more from the hour.

The team teaching has allowed one teacher in each wing to take time to train quite intensively in the literacy hour methods. We believe that the staff have to be enthusiastic about their work, and the children too seem to be keen on the literacy hour. We have had to change assembly to first thing in the morning, to fit in the hour, and when Brigid says, 'Have a really good day and enjoy your literacy hour', they cheer 'Yes!' The literacy hour was set up fully here, from the first day of the autumn term, in every wing. Natalie, Joanne, Joe and Luke commented:

> Yes, it is good.
> It's helping our reading and our handwriting skills so when we get older we'll know a lot and then we can get a good job.
> When we get into the big school we'll know lots.
> We're learning about phonemes and phonics and spelling and rhyming words.

The children like the newness of the literacy hour and the structure of part of the session with the whole class then going off to do small group activities, which they are very good at, they move and settle quickly. It is good that there are lots of glossy new books and new ideas and activities and equipment, which should keep up their interest. The whole idea is for them to progress, so when the staff have assessed the children's different abilities we'll move them on in the literacy hour, because here we work on all the children having maximum access to their level of work.

Because we have changed the two reading and writing rooms into literacy rooms, this could limit the range of activities available to the children. So that we can maintain the broad curriculum and not shut that down, we keep the other three rooms and the PE options open. The other 60 children are spread in four rooms in smaller groups than before each morning. Unexpectedly, we now find that we pay more attention to maths and science.

During the 20 minutes of group work in the literacy hour, there are up to five groups of about six children in each room, and the teacher works with one of the groups while other groups work independently. There are enough learning support staff to work with groups as well as individual children, depending on the needs of the wing and the children, to support the differentiated learning with, say, a game or a quiz. All children are included in the first 15 minutes of the big book and we're working to enable all of them to do that. All the children are used to sitting on the floor round the teacher, and this is a good way to look at the big book. The older ones sometimes use text on an overhead projector.

Most of the children share in the first part, reading the big book. Some may not stay for the second part, the sentence or word level session for the next 15 minutes, it depends on the activity, while they all work on their independent group work. We try to make sure the children with profound difficulties take part in sensory activities linked to literacy, such as working with sand shapes or paint, dough or letter shapes, or sorting and matching. Probably not every child with special needs would spend the whole hour on literacy but they would spend some part of that hour. Some of them, after they have done their sentence and word activity, might join the more profoundly disabled ones in sensory activities.

Are more able children held back? No, they don't seem to be, the idea of the big book work is to enthuse children about books, to delight in books as well as teaching specific skills. The hour is divided into short sections, and it is up to the skilful teacher to ensure that all children are working at their own level. The principle of this teaching is based on entitlement and equality, access to literacy for everyone. We don't yet know if the literacy hour methods have changed the way the children learn other subjects. However, it usually takes children from the early years wing about half a term to settle into Key Stage 1, and this term they have been quicker, perhaps because of the more formal start to the day. The reception children do a slightly shorter literacy hour as well, and they seem to enjoy having fun with words and stories.

As it is so important for the staff to feel confident and enthusiastic about the literacy hour we have set up a literacy team. There is a Literacy Coordinator with a funding allowance point in each wing. They have to see that the literacy hour and the resources work well, and they get the staff to share in talking about what works well. Three staff went together on an intensive training course. Newham LEA literacy consultants run courses and have visited Cleves and approve of our approaches. All the staff have been doing training in the school with the literacy hour toolkit from the DfEE (Department for Education and Employment).

The training pack is very precise, giving staff knowledge about teaching techniques and clearer understanding about how children learn to read, so that they can learn through working with the children. The challenge is, whatever activity we do, how can we make it inclusive, for children of different abilities and also for boys and girls, and children from different ethnic backgrounds. It is important that we make inclusive approaches work during the literacy hour and we have managed to do that relatively easily. The things we worried about losing we're not sure we have lost. For example, we have to work now with chronological, single-year groups during the hour, but the children still work in mixed-age groups at other times. Before, the two-year groups worked together all the time and you can have very skilled children in Year 1 doing Year 2 activities.

Our dilemma when the 45 minutes of maths begins is whether we shut down the rest of the curriculum while we do maths and literacy, or try to keep the other options open. Or do we have four maths sessions running through the day? That is a lot for the teacher doing two weeks of maths to provide. Although the curriculum has changed to four core subjects, we are maintaining the same level of art and music, history and geography.

Reading and learning in the early years

Learning English in an inclusive school

Inclusive teaching and learning approaches which involve children with all kinds of abilities can also work well with staff and children who are new to the school, and to those who speak English as an additional language.

Lara, English as an additional language teacher

I worked in a more usual kind of school for six years before coming to Cleves. Teaching English as an additional language is much easier in this school, because there is already a lot of sensory work, and signing. Children can become more involved from the start in a closer way. With the team teaching here, that means I can suggest ideas to other staff and they see that as helpful. They are open and ready and quick to pick up new ideas. They don't see that as at all threatening or challenging to them. My main purpose here is to work in partnership with all the teachers. It can be harder in schools where the classroom is very much the individual teacher's territory, and then you come in and say 'Can we work together? Can I share everything with you?' If they are not used to that, it can be very difficult and you have to go in very gently. But here they enjoy working in teams, as partners. They are used to sharing ideas together. At the beginning of each day, we each set up our own area, it might be maths or finding out, and then we go and see each other's areas and make suggestions.

All the areas are set out so beautifully, they are so stimulating and attractive to help the children to want to learn. In more traditional schools you don't usually get the older classes set out like the early years rooms. At my previous school, I didn't have a sensory area, or children with disabilities, though I did have some with behaviour problems. At Cleves there are people coming in and out all the time, visitors and other people, and it is so flexible, and warm and welcoming. It is all open. You walk through the door and everything is out on display. You don't have to go to find a folder about what you are doing.

This school includes children with severe learning difficulties in all the activities. Everyone is valued here, I think that's the big difference. Children who have recently arrived in England and do not yet speak much English are included as much as everyone else. They are encouraged to use English and their first language as well. I thought that would be a big job for me to get my colleagues to allow them to do this, give them opportunities to use their first language too, but it is not so here. There are displays here in first and second languages, and it is the ethos of the whole school, not just a few individual teachers who might do that. I hear children speaking their first language together very freely, and teachers often looking for other children and staff who can speak the same language.

Here, it is about equality, no matter who you are, what you look like, what you do, we are all the same, we all have something to contribute. It is very noticeable, very striking here. I was amazed to see how children work alongside other children who need helping out. They do not stare at a child with a severe disability, they play happily alongside them. And they are so careful in what they are doing: 'Here you are, let's give you a hand, I'll help you with that colouring, you are doing this well.' You hear those kinds of conversations. I would like my own children to come to a school like this one, where they value and help each other so much, and where people are so used to working together.

Teachers do not think, 'It is just my area', it is everyone's area. Observations and assessments are done together. Everyone contributes to marking all the children's books. All the time, the staff are showing the children how they would like them to share and work together. We do use competition in some of the activities. We do encourage them to do their very best, in a healthy way, to compete against their own best, without trying to over-emphasise success. But we do celebrate their achievements.

Continuity

To ensure consistent teaching, and to help agency and student staff, there are posters in the wings about methods and equipment, for example:

In the art area there should be provision for:

- painting
- tactile/sensory activities: dough, plasticine, clay, spaghetti, sequins, porridge, cornflour
- range of drawing tools and paper – pencils, crayons, felt-tips, chalks
- cutting activities (ground rules need to be clear)
- sticking/gluing activities (*please* ensure that you use the right glue for the materials, i.e. water-based glue will stick paper, you do *not* need to use white glue or Pritt stick!)
- model making – using a range of equipment
- challenging activity (can be from above list) incorporating other areas, equipment, where necessary, e.g. colour mixing can be extended/continued by the use of pyramids, kaleidoscopes, colour sticks
- sand – wet and dry if possible – can be in sand tray, small drawer
- water – in sink or tray, with additions – colour, sequins, bubbles, etc.

Remember issues of accessibility – levels that activities are placed at are crucial.

Children with learning difficulties

Each wing has a curriculum support teacher who coordinates all the work for children with special needs. They organise the Individual Education Plans (IEPs). A few children have very clearly identified support mainly linked to one person, but our aim is to make all our children as independent as possible. Some have shared support to help to develop their learning. It is very much a flexible system. Children who have come from other schools where they had one-to-one support find it very difficult for that support to be changed. But slowly they have adapted to this system and become much more independent. Some found it difficult at first because of the big spaces and the amount of people, the noise of people talking in pairs and groups, and the colour and movement, and many different activities. One reason that, for example, children on the autistic spectrum are referred to a special school is the belief that they need quiet, secure routines and surroundings which help to make them calmer and less distracted, but we have found they soon settle in here and do well.

Lyn, teacher responsible for computers and IT

Computers are used generally to support work in all the curriculum areas. There are also devices to help the children with special needs. We make up concept keyboards for them with specific words that they use. They have pictures which come on the screen when they press them. If they have a certain need that requires a computer, it is usually written into their statement and the LEA has a responsibility to supply it. The IT assessment unit in the borough decides what they need.

The aims of independent learning

Most parents say they are very pleased with the learning methods at Cleves and their child's progress. A few have concerns, at first. For example:

A parent's comments

I am happy with this school. The open plan is nice in the nursery, but I would prefer a classroom setting, I think children need to be taught discipline, they need to have that sit-down routine. My older son is a studious child, he likes reading but he found it very difficult because there's children coming and going while he's trying to work. They say that's because children in this school have to have their own self-discipline, and I can see the benefits in that. I don't think the open plan is a bad thing. It's just my preference. There are certain children that have to be told every five minutes, 'You haven't finished your work.' With my older son it was fine because he sits down and gets on with it. But with my younger one it will be a completely different ball game because he's never still, always off, it will be a problem for him. He's sporty and very active, you have to coax him to eat, everything – it's always a big job with him. It's not that he's naughty, it's his character. I don't feel they should be disciplined all the time to make them work, but that once they know it's a classroom setting they come in and get on with it. Whereas here, there are so many distractions to sidetrack them. But here there are so many other pluses and benefits.

In reply to this concern, one teacher commented:

Certain children clearly need a routine. And this freedom cannot happen without responsibility, but by putting children in a strict classroom you are taking away from them the chance to learn to be free people with responsibility. You're stopping that from happening until a later stage, and that's like running away. I would try to work this through with a child by setting clear boundaries, until the child was ready to take on the free responsibility. This system does expect a lot of the children. And they can learn to do that partly by seeing how the others manage. Our policy is that it's not 'do as you want', it's much deeper, more sophisticated than that. It's trying to encourage them to be in charge of their own being.

Some children have to have their day planned for them. Responsibility for who they are, their learning and their behaviour is very much emphasised. You could have low expectations in this system, and in any system, and let them get away with things. But you can have high expectations and watch them carefully, we have enough staff here to do that, and say to them, 'This is not good enough, you need to go on doing it, you haven't finished yet.' It depends how you approach the child, and talk about the things we don't like to do, and the things we have to do. But it is still hard, with such large numbers of children and you have to work very hard. It is exhausting, but here I'm tired but happy and that's a big difference from my last school where I was tired and depressed about my work. I had to fight for power all the time there, but I don't need to here, it's enjoyable.

Chapter 4
Being friends and being equals: relationships and rules

The principle of inclusion

Principles of Cleves School:

- all children have the right to access to the whole school curriculum;
- children and adults learn best in an environment where they feel valued, accepted and respected;
- discrimination undermines both perpetrators' and victims' ability to achieve: our curriculum, relationships and organisation must challenge this and present positive images and practices;
- all adults and children who enter our school have equal worth.

Brigid

Schools have to decide on their purpose. and look at their management and organisation to see if they meet their purpose, and how you enable that to take place. For example, inclusion has to happen in everything we say and do. It can't just be added on, and that is why it shouldn't be called integration. Inclusion is more powerful, because it means you take the needs of all children, particularly those who are most vulnerable, that might be because of their gender or their circumstances or their learning needs, or whatever, and you say 'How does the institution enable that child to come to school and be happy and feel "Oh it's great, I'll have some good fun at school today and I'm going to learn at the same time with my friends."?' It is about how you organise ordinary things like assemblies and lunch times, access to equipment, furniture, basic things, on one level. Then on the next level you say, 'What do we do to create a climate whereby everybody is accepted and valued?' That will include doing things like positive self-esteem and circle time, and cooperative collaborative learning, and discipline which is about relationships and not conflict.

Cleves is about making sure there is an entitlement curriculum. It is curriculum-driven. You can set up lots of nice opportunities, but they will not work if during their learning time children are made to feel bad about their learning, or feel criticised instead of encouraged. Inclusion is about tolerance and flexibility, about not judging the child or family but working with them. It's essential to have that positive relationship with them where they'll come and talk to us and feel okay about that. If they are really angry and upset, it's all right for us to say to them, 'I can see you're angry and upset, let's sit down and talk about it.'

With principles, you have to set up quite a clear vision of the school so that every one can have a clear view too. So we make it very clear to parents that any child is admitted. And staff were recruited on that principle as well. It was not something we surprised them with on their first day.

It was a matter of setting the boundaries of behaviour and relationships. Those ten points of an effective school (Sammons *et al.* 1995) are very good, about being clear, and knowing what the leadership means and what the aims are, I think we keep to them, though we may interpret them rather differently. For example, if you are going to do PE warm-ups with a child with physical disabilities, then you are going to think about doing them on the ground, not standing up. Or at lunch-time, we have people who eat packed lunches and school dinners together, and it is okay to sit and gossip in the dining hall, you don't all have to be herded in and out at the same time.

A whole-ability-range school

Many adults are concerned that bringing children with disabilities and difficulties into mainstream schools risks harming them with unkindness and rejection from other children. Cleves shows, as happens in other schools (Lewis 1995a; Alderson and Goodey 1998) that when the adults encourage them, the children tend to be very active in making inclusion work. Some parents commented on the children's responses:

> The children see special needs children every day so they don't grow up and take the mickey out of them, and they tend to help out with them.
> When I was little I would stop and stare at people with special needs, but my children don't do that, they see them around the school and I like that. In the community there are a lot of people with something wrong with them and the school helps the children to mingle with them and sort of accept them outside as well as in the school.

When some Year 6 children talked about inclusion, Delicia and Sarah gave examples of teaching about probability, with methods that are appropriate to any ability level, and which reinforce inclusion.

> **Delicia:** I think it is helpful having us all mixed together, because the slow people know something that you don't know and you know what they don't know, and we can all have a chat together. They might not be able to talk to each other in the same way, but you're always allowed to talk in your own way, you either use sign language or anything you want, because we learn sign language. We could photocopy the alphabet to go in the book.

> **Sarah:** In the morning we was doing this 'moving on up to a new school' book, and my friend Lisa was a bit slow and my other friend Emma was a bit slow and I was helping Lisa and she was helping Emma with reading, and sometimes they needed words and that. They did it on their own but

Learning and Inclusion: The Cleves School Experience

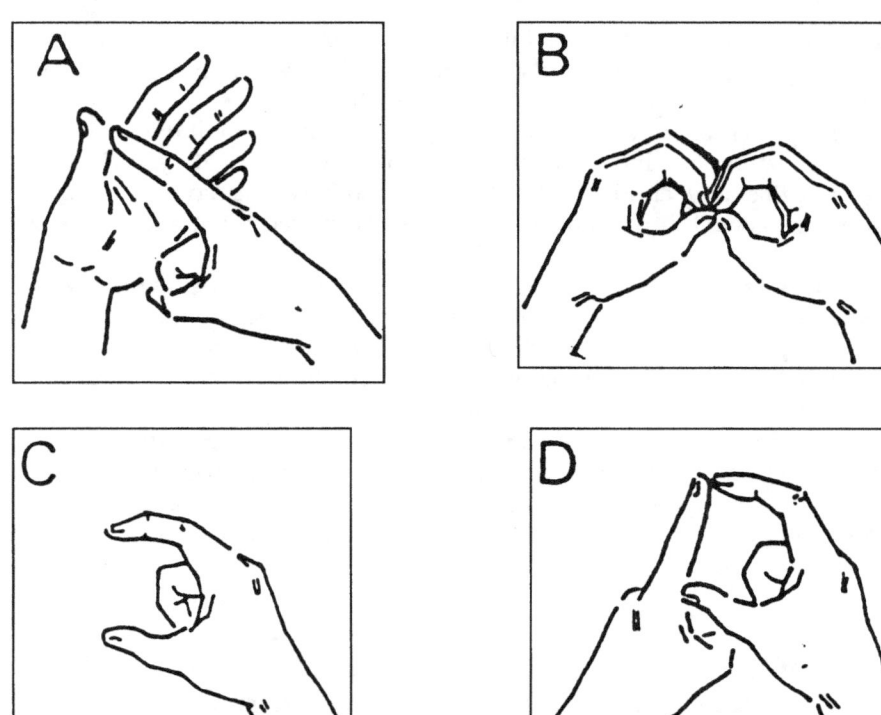

From the early years, children use the British two-handed finger spelling alphabet

we helped if they needed something. We had to make our own front cover and we had to help them with that.

Delicia: In one area we've got maths for special needs, about what's a half and what's a quarter, and last week we was learning about percentages and probability – if it's likely, unlikely, impossible to happen. Is it possible that a dragon would come to your school? And we had to make our own ones up, and I said, 'It's possible that I'll get knocked over in the week.' And yesterday a car skidded up the back of my leg, that's never happened before. It was just a guess and I got it right. And we talked about 'Is it possible it's going to rain today?' and my teacher explained about winning the lottery.

One boy throws things around, but Patrick controls him. He's just like a friend to him, if he holds him by one hand he stops it, it's really weird. And he's very good at calming down some of the others.

Respecting and celebrating difference

Mary, a teacher

I chose to work in a multicultural school because I'm interested in social justice, I believe every human needs to be valued and accepted and loved and treated as a genuine being. I feel there is a great sense of spirituality here, even though it is not explicit, a sense of underlying belief. A lot of what the teachers are doing here is RE, more than they are aware. However, we also need explicitly to teach the world faiths, accept the differences and also value the similarities. Many of our children go to mosque after school and learn the Koran. So the teachers don't need to feel they have to be the RE expert, because many of the children are experts. The curriculum, therefore, is set up round that, a first-hand, person-centred experiential approach that celebrates our diverse society. It feeds tolerance and anti-racism. That's much easier to do here than in a school with one main faith where there might be ignorance and prejudice.

I give people in other wings ideas if they want them, they use the yearly plan for each wing. We have assembly and collective worship in our wing once a week. There is a theme for the week for the school, taking note of festivals in the main faiths: friendship, patience, understanding, journeys, diversity, community. We did friendship-building for a term, it is much easier to do it in a friendly school like this one. In the last week of term we will do moving on. I try to link it to the school year. Assemblies in the wing are very free. It's always active. We brainstorm, play a game, and the children might present things they have done. We might have short meditation with space for them to opt out. I might say, 'Close your eyes and think: How was this for you? Where do you link it in your own life?' Or we might read a poem. Assemblies are a time of celebrating being together, and to reflect and respond spiritually to a given message.

A parent

I'm a Jehovah's Witness and the staff respect that. For instance, birthday times my children do not sit in on the happy birthday song. They go to another group where it isn't sung. The school is nice because they accept that. My seven-year-old understands. He can quote scriptures to you and explain to you why he doesn't celebrate those things. But obviously when they're younger they just see other children joining in and though they might start to sing, the teacher will get the child and say 'No, Mummy doesn't like that', and they are following on what I would expect at home. And obviously there are others of different religions, different sects, and they cater for that too. I'm very happy about that, definitely.

Joy

I think a lot of the children's friendliness and respect is modelling and starts with all the staff getting involved with everybody – picking things up off the floor, doing dinner duty, sorting things out with them, and taking what they say seriously. And then there isn't a hierarchy with the staff. We've all got a role. We're all doing our best, and working at it. And we respect and value everybody's different role. It's not, 'You'll do the washing up because you're the learning support assistant.' So the team leader is equally to be found washing up and making tea and dealing with the nappies. We all have a hand in everything. The coordinators for each subject advise and give ideas, but they are not seen as experts, they'll say 'try this'. When we wrote, say, the RE document, we were a mixed group; staff from every wing, teachers and others were involved. Everyone took ownership. So I think the children see that, and they perceive the staff as being equally respected.

Some children are ready to be friends, but some children at first find it really difficult to share another adult with 15 other children, or to share a toy. It's an enormous lesson to learn. We spend a lot of time reasoning it through, giving them the language to negotiate, rather than quarrelling, and I think that threads right through the school, we all have to be committed to that because otherwise, when they get big, you've got bigger problems.

We work hard at giving children the words to explain what happened, trying not to make assumptions about who was in the wrong, and working out with their help what is the solution to this problem. 'You both want the same toy, what are we going to do?' We hope in the end they'll come up with an idea, 'Well, you can have it for two minutes and then I'll have it for two minutes, and maybe we'll play together.' In some places you see the toy just taken off the child and put on a high shelf. You're just using your power then, and behaving in a way you don't want them to behave. We use every kind of difficulty as a learning opportunity. We teach through all those things. We think that's a very good use of our time. Most of the time we achieve, but sometimes we fall down on it.

When you are in a big team, if one person gets involved in sorting out things with the children, a colleague can take over her role to allow that to happen. It needs all the staff to keep reading situations, and to intervene where necessary when you can support a colleague, so they can make sure that what is happening is fair.

Inclusion in many details

Displays

Displays around the school:

- reflect what is going on in the community, keeping visitors and members of the school up to date with events and advice sessions, etc.
- represent the range of languages spoken in our community
- show positive images of all groups of people
- show the range of activities and achievements of the children, displayed attractively and informatively at a variety of levels. This includes the use of artefacts, languages and scripts, three-dimensional art and clear labelling.

The books and pictures in the school, as in many schools, are chosen carefully for the messages they give, as well as for their other educational aspects. These include positive images of people around the world. We look for stories which challenge conflict and discrimination, and those which are about the sadness of rejection and happiness in reconciliation, like the ugly duckling story. *The Rainbow Fish* is about a fish who found friendship and happiness by giving away his brightly coloured scales. We use these kinds of stories for reading, discussions, drama and art. With the early years children, we made a long collage with sentences from The Rainbow Fish on a background of sea, and pictures of the stages of the story. Everyone can share in sticking on watery waves or fish scales, so that all the individual children and their work are gathered together through the process of making the display. Another collage with gold and silver stars and tinsel on black paper has the words of *Twinkle Twinkle Little Star* also in gold and silver, and photographs of children signing the words with Makaton sign language. Another example, from very many details, is having two-seater bikes in the early years garden, so that children with different strength and ability can ride around together.

Joy

The climate is changing slowly on inclusion. You see low level buses and ramps into buildings. It is like gender or race equality, coming to be achieved. By now, nearly all our disabled children started here in the early years. We aim towards including children so that they take part in all the activities and mix fully with the other children right through the school.

Clothing

Brigid

There are always a few parents who prefer to have uniforms and we discussed this at one parents' meeting. In Newham, there is no uniform grant, and a mother who, I thought, was very courageous said, 'I'm on benefits and I've got five children. How on earth am I going to afford a school uniform?' At this school, there are children with different kinds of body shapes, children who are learning to be mobile, to feed themselves, and to be toileted. They would need five or six sets of uniform.

Uniform is a governor decision and at the next governor meeting I presented a document which looking at the issues: children with needs, the celebration of difference, respecting cultural values and dress patterns, celebrating the individual. With children at primary age, especially, each one needs to be respected as a creative human being, and when you look at the playground in the summer it is enriching to see everyone wearing different kinds of clothes which are suitable to the task of learning. We do not have to spend any time dealing with children who do not arrive in uniform, and we do not have the disagreements which can arise between the staff and children in some schools about uniform. Although uniform is said to encourage a sense of corporate identity, you can get that sense of identity from the institution as a whole, the feelings and relationships in the school, through taking part in what everyone is doing, and not just from a piece of clothing. After discussion, all the governors agreed that the school would not have a uniform.

Mixing between age groups

Joy

We have sensory equipment in all the wings, for the oldest ones too, and for anyone who perhaps feels a bit distressed, they get engaged in some tactile activity. Here you can dabble with everything and everything has equal status, early years with 2B, that's very important. Sometimes if the older ones get strung up, they'll come to work with the younger children for a while, and feel responsible and respected. They might be sent here, but it's to protect them, and it's an occasion when I can say, 'Well done, we relied on you today'. And some children need that kind of boost, they can go back and say they did really well and by then they've got over whatever upset them.

In many schools I've worked in, the early years are seen as a separate entity and no one ever goes in, and it's not part of the 'big' school. But here, students work throughout the school, staff interact, the older ones might come down here, the little ones go up to see bigger ones.

Friends of different ages and ability

Sinsi: We've got friends in other wings. We like playing with the little ones. The soft play room is in their wing and we like going there. You've got to work very hard to be allowed to go there. Sometimes we play with the nursery children, and sometimes with other children who just turn up.

Patrick: Yes, I've got lots of friends in other wings. My brother's four years younger than me and I like playing with him and his friends.

Sarah: Sometimes we go to the sensory room. The helpers who look after the disabled children choose us to go with them. Donna's friend has special needs, she's like kind of slow, and when we take turns in reading at base time she wants to do it. She has got the right to do it, and she can choose a friend to help her. She was reading a novel and I helped her with it, and when she took it home I helped her at home.

Tidying up

Joy

Clearing up is another way we all work equally. The children can work with so many activities and resources at once because everyone helps to tidy up. That is never a punishment, but a dignified task for everyone. We are all responsible for clearing up, it's a communal thing. You might find children putting away Lego or something they've never played with that afternoon. If adults put it away for them, that would rob them of experiences and opportunities, to sort into sets, to be helpful, to feel good that they're caring about other people and their environment. While it's much easier and quicker to do it yourself, it takes a lot of energy to direct children and help them to notice what needs to be done. I don't find any difference between girls and boys, or culturally or anything, in helping to clear up, I think they can be equally good or equally poor at it. We have checklists on the walls for everyone to use.

The two checklists show how new staff can quickly see how the tidying up routines work.

> **Areas/equipment to check in early years wing during and at the end of the session/day**
>
> - pencils/writing equipment sharpened, tops on, dried-up pens disposed of
>
> - all paper piles tidied and topped up – for writing, painting, number work
>
> - paint brushes, pots and lids washed as appropriate – paint-drying area cleared, if possible, and wiped, aprons wiped/washed
>
> - water and sand toys washed and trays prepared
>
> - puzzles completed, books mended
>
> - home corner equipment sorted correctly
>
> - construction kits in correct containers
>
> - outside toys tidied and/or put away at the end of the day
>
> - hygiene room and kitchen tidy – all cups washed, milk in the fridge, juice in bottles, drinks table wiped, washing cleared
>
> - paper towels in holders, paper in toilets
>
> - toilets mopped (11.30 a.m.)
>
> - nappy bucket empty.

Most of these jobs can, and should be done by, or with, the children during the session, as part of taking responsibility for what they have done and tidying up after they have finished.

The learning environment: a checklist for equality of access

Preparation:

- Is there scope for group, paired and individual work?
- Have you left enough room for rollators and for people to move about easily?
- Are activities on different levels?
- Is every activity given equal status by its position?
- Was the activity out yesterday – how has it been developed?
- Is there a large enough range of equipment?
- Can every child in the wing be challenged in this area?
- Are the equipment and resources ready to use?
- Is the equipment presented creatively?
- Is there enough room to work at all the activities?
- Is the equipment stored in an accessible way for all children?
- Are labels and instructions big enough, clear enough and simple enough – using symbols, pictures and words?
- Has the area been re-serviced for the next session?

During session:

- Is the area kept tidy and re-serviced?
- Does every child get equal time?
- Are you ensuring that each child is on-task?
- Are you aware of what all the children are doing?
- Do you have enough extension activities on hand?
- Are staff fully deployed and sure of their roles?
- Is there a mixture of children involved (gender, race, need)?
- Is group work cooperative?
- Are you supportive of the children's initiatives?
- Are you covered when you leave?
- Do the children know where to store completed work?
- Have you and the child evaluated the activity and completed the diary?
- Do they know where to go next?

End of session:

- Have they been warned that the session is ending?
- Is everyone equally involved in tidying up – do they know the expectations?
- Is it fast?
- Are instructions clear?
- Is the equipment complete and put away in its correct place?
- Is there a way of tasks being continued in the next session?
- Have you completed the observation file?
- Have you pulled out the trolleys and picked up everything off the floor?
- Are the children ready to go on to their next activity or to go home?

Cooperation

Cooperation is helped by having wings instead of four separate classes. The children see the staff working as a team and see team work as a principle across the school.

Together
Each
Achieves
More

We do a lot of group work on collaboration and cooperation. The notion of inclusion is about cooperation and not competition. Say some people make noises in assembly or in your group story, you have to be tolerant about that and think that is okay. We do parachute work and games that encourage cooperation. There is quite a lot in the climate of the school about not being selfish, and being fair, these are all facets of the overall aims of the school.

We encourage learning all together in mixed ability groups (see Chapter 3). The approach is to say let's share our skills and learn from each other, and everyone has skills to offer. Separate ability groupings can imply that some people are worth more than others, so we avoid them. At one time, equal opportunities as about everyone being equal, and that was an important stage, although now we see that equality is about people having an equal entitlement while celebrating their differences, instead of seeing these as a problem. All children are human beings, some of them happen to have a difficulty, and we look at ways they can just have some help to get on with their lives.

Training to teach children with special needs

We are quite keen to start from the child and assess each one's needs, rather than go by the book. We think about health and safety, and about dignity and privacy and respect – like who should and should not change a child in terms of children's rights. We do a lot of work on self-esteem. For example, we had a training session on advocacy for disabled people, it was challenging and it is ongoing. We have to keep up to date constantly, in things like language and the way you treat people, keep revisiting ideas with individual children, and their personal targets. We try to look from the child's standpoint, as opposed to a pre-set approach.

Debbie, deputy head and SENCO

> We have lots of in-service day training. All London boroughs, Newham in particular, have a high staff turnover, and we also have some agency staff. Some of the staff have done special needs courses, but many of the staff come without much experience and soon become very experienced in working with all the children. They move on to other schools with that experience. When the school opened we had many sessions, at least one a week, about special needs, the staff who have stayed on here know a great deal. We don't tend to recruit people because they have specialised

Key Stage 1 sensory learning with fir-cones, jelly, tomato sauce and flour textures

in this field, but people tend to come to work here so that they can learn about it.

We cover the whole range of needs including behaviour problems, we accept any child who is on the Code of Practice. If staff want advice or ideas or any information about any child they'll come to me. Children with Down's syndrome were the first to be integrated in Newham. When there was publicity about this new school taking in children with many more needs I was very interested and applied to come here. My background is early years in mainstream schools. When children come into the school, I see them as children first. Some learn at a slower rate, or have a range of difficulties that they have to overcome. I think I use the teaching techniques here which I have always used in mainstream schools – whatever will help a child to learn, I will use that.

Staff who come to this school realise the mix of children and what they will be expected to do, though it is not overt. I always show the toilets to visitors. Lots of our children are on toilet programmes, having to be taken to the toilet at certain times, and some are in nappies, and you deal with accidents as they arise. In some schools, they think only the support staff should deal with that. But I expect all staff in the school, permanent and on long-term supply, to deal with those kind of issues. If a learning assistant or a nursery nurse is not around, and a child needs changing, and you can't wait, you have to deal with it yourself. You can't leave a child needing help. What is important is that it is a person that the child knows well and is happy with. If not, then it is much better to wait until the right person can help, but it doesn't happen that often. We exclude short-term supply teachers from this, because we don't know them and they don't know us well.

We also exclude male staff, for their own protection. We talked about it in great detail, with quite heated discussions. We were in a very mixed group, from different cultures, different religions, drawing up our health and hygiene policy. Lots of us said that we would be quite happy for Steve, the only man present, to change our children, but a few people didn't want that because he was a man, and a Muslim nursery nurse would not want him to change a girl, or even a boy. I also spoke to some parents I knew well. They said they would be quite happy because they knew Steve, but you can't decide on the grounds that one person can but another, who you know or trust less well as an individual, can't. A child can be abused equally by a woman as by a man, but it is to protect the man against the risk of allegations. For some of our children, toileting is part of their education and must be done with privacy and dignity and it helps that there are toilets and changing spaces in every wing.

I don't think it is essential to go on courses about disabilities although you do need background knowledge to draw on. I've used lots of people for that, working really closely with the preschool home visiting team teachers, for example, and if I don't know something I'll ask them. We find ongoing training most helpful, drawing on people like the school nurse, educational psychologist, physiotherapist, occupational therapists (OTs) who work in the school. They do some training with us and they come in to work with individual children. Physios come twice a week, but OTs work on a case-by-case approach.

When learning support assistants have to give intimate care, such as with toileting, it is vital that they know how to do it well, that they are respected and supported, and that the child is happy to be cared for by them. Support staff can greatly influence how happy disabled children are in mainstream school (Alderson and Goodey 1998). An advantage of having numbers of disabled children, and therefore of support staff, in mainstream schools is that the staff can help and learn from one another. They are less likely to feel isolated or less respected by other staff, and if a child feels unhappy with one or two of them, there will probably be others whom the child does like.

Non-exclusion

Debbie

We have a non-exclusion policy in all our activities. Children are not taken out of the wing for any reason, unless it is agreed with me or their curriculum support teacher. All the wings have a quieter room where you can work with children. For example, Jo, our physio, came in today and sat in the early years book room with one of our children, and her mum and a nursery nurse, to do a review.

I had a discussion last week with an occupational therapist. She wanted to take a child out of the wing to do an assessment in the ball pool in the foyer. I said, 'That's fine if you do that with a group of children.' She said she wanted to work with her on her own. So I said, 'That doesn't give a true picture of what Elizabeth can do, because in school Elizabeth is always with other children, never on her own with an adult, or with one she doesn't know particularly well, or on her own outside her wing.' We then went to the wing, and I showed her spaces where she could work with Elizabeth. She wanted to go into a separate smaller room in the wing. I said, 'That's fine as long as you leave the door open and other children can come in and out normally.' In the end I said, 'It would be better if you work in the reading room. It's a quiet space where children will be around and you will get normal responses from Elizabeth.' So we are quite firm, making sure that everyone here follows inclusive policies. Most people are really flexible, and work in the system, in the wings, once they see the school.

Health care as part of education which increases inclusion

The aims are to increase children's social competence and integration into the school and into society. The methods are for all the staff concerned, with the children and parents, to work closely and equally, learning from each other with mutual respect including the visiting therapists and outside teachers from the LEA's Learning Support Services.

Debbie

Speech and language therapists usually work with one or two children, or with groups. If they write a programme for a child, they are not here every day so it would be one of the school staff who does the programme and it is important that the speech therapist passes that information and the techniques and methods on to the member of staff. So we encourage them to train and work with staff about particular aspects of the children's programmes. They liaise with the curriculum support teacher but also with all the rest of the staff. They assess children and offer their expert advice about what children need and then they teach us programmes which anyone can use.

For example, one girl has problems with saliva control, and the speech therapist showed us control activities like using brushes, getting her to swallow, making different mouth shapes, and chewing and swallowing, blowing, a whole list of activities to do with her. And it is useful to know that for other children. We decided to try the programme with another boy in early years, to see if it works, and then, if it doesn't, we'll talk to the speech therapists, but it does seem to be working.

One boy was having difficulty feeding. The speech therapist worked with the person doing his programmes. She suggested better seating positions and liquidising his food slightly more. That has helped to improve his feeding skills, as well as providing ways of ensuring that he doesn't choke on his food, which is so important. She also spoke to the staff member about going slowly, and giving him time to respond, to wait for signs from him that he wanted more food. He's always loved having his food, but he had just had an operation on his legs and was more uncomfortable, and still adjusting to coming back to school, so maybe he had taken a few steps back after making a lot of progress. So in a way we had to go a few steps back with him in every area, in order to move on.

The OTs focus on seating for children, and hand function and care skills, with reports for the parents and teachers with ideas for them to carry out. Jo, our physio, shows two or three members of staff the daily programme of (muscle) stretches. The staff will notice changes in children – whether they are getting looser and more mobile, or tighter, or stiffer, or having difficulty, or are uncomfortable. They'll tell the curriculum support teacher, who will talk to Jo the next time she comes in, and ask for advice.

If a child finds the exercises or the standing frames painful, we'll work with children and physios. Usually you can build up children's tolerance. If a child can understand or can say that he doesn't like doing something, you can say, we'll do this for ten minutes then you can choose what you want to do, something you really enjoy like the soft play, and gradually you build up his ability to use the standing frame. We tell children why they need to use these things, and we tell other children when they ask –

about the need to build up strength in their legs, and that it's nice to stand up because you can see lots of different things. We wouldn't do things that hurt children or make them uncomfortable, and if it did, we would always refer straight back to the physio – it's maybe the way the stretching is being done. Most children are very cooperative. With the younger ones, it is a matter of building up tolerance and, say, using the standing frame at favourite things everyday. One little girl didn't like the standing frame at all, so we started with her almost lying down, on her front and gradually every week we built it up a little bit, and up and up. But she would always play with the water which she loved. At first it was only for ten minutes, or as long as she was happy. We always made sure some of her really good friends were there.

We try to fit physio as unobtrusively as possible into the ordinary day, fitting in with what is best for the child. You can look at their diary. If you know they have stretching and then half an hour in the standing frame, you might do it first thing in the morning, but give them a bit of choice about negotiating it, although within the limits that you have to do it some time. Some of the children can verbalise their feelings, and with others we have to read their signals. Even children who are not verbal have other ways of showing you that they don't like something or they don't want to do something. Reassuring them, and seeing they are as comfortable as possible, all matter.

But, whatever we think about it, children have to do these things. It will improve their physical skills and their access to the world and to school. Once you know children well, you can read from the movements of their eyes, facial expressions, tension in their body, all of those things. You can communicate with every child in this school however profound their disabilities, once you know them and you build up a relationship. One little girl settled here really well, but she doesn't give out many signals. The staff are getting to know her, gradually coming to read the signals – 'I need a drink, I'm unhappy, I'm happy.' Her face doesn't tell us much unless she's really distressed, but staff say they are beginning to notice slight changes in her facial expression. Maybe it is a mixture of her developing more expressions and the staff learning to read them more sensitively, as they get to know her. We think that if there's a problem there's a solution, a way round it if we talk to enough of the people concerned. But I do encounter lots of parents who have come up against lots of brick walls. Ones who are keen for their children to attend local schools, but have come up against toilet training, so their child is rejected as not toilet trained.

With toilet training, we don't make a big thing out of it – except when they do perform, when we go 'Great! Wonderful!' and they get a smiley face on the toilet chart. But otherwise we try to keep it low key and just part of normal routine. At the most we would sit a child in the toilet for a few minutes.

Our learning support staff are very good and skilled and they know much more about some of the children and their needs than the teachers do. The borough does courses mainly for teachers, but we encourage the support staff to come on all the teachers' training days, and they are paid to do that. New teachers coming into the school can learn a lot from them. I say to everyone, 'The knowledge you have got is there to be shared. If I don't know something, I ask someone. Nobody knows everything.' People who come new to school say to me 'You know everything.' I say, 'No, I know the children and through my early years experience and being here six years I've built up the knowledge.'

Each half term we review our IEPs with parents if they come in. I send a copy of the evaluated IEP with the new one saying 'Have a look at it, see what you think, if there's anything you want to talk about then let me know.' They are written in English and several staff in school speak other languages. The parents often say they understand, even when things might not be clear, so I always get someone who speaks Urdu or Bengali to ring them, so that they are getting a good clear message. If parents come to reviews, then I'll get a translator if they need one, and parents can add much more into the meeting. The IEPs are shared with all of the staff each half term, and the learning support staff on that wing are paid to come to the after school meeting because they are key people.

Treating children equally

Staff and parents in many LEAs are concerned that special needs budgets in mainstream schools are spent generally, instead of directly on the children concerned. Treating children as equals involves sharing resources, except when a child needs certain extra equipment or support, like a computer for a child who has almost no movement at all when, as already mentioned, the LEA pays for this separately.

Brigid

We put all the funding as one budget and we don't say £20,000 for this child and £5,000 for that child. We look at the needs of each child and each wing, and that drives the staffing. This year we have one learning support assistant too many, but because she are part of our community and we can still afford her, we keep her to provide extra cover, which is a good thing for everyone. We encourage all the children to work as hard as they can, whatever their difficulties.

Some of our children are very preoccupied with rituals. Then we ask: What do you need to do to enable a child not to be distressed? A degree of ritual is important for all of us, like the way we get up in the morning. With one boy, we organised his day, but within sessions he's allowed to have treats and freedoms. When he was five, we found he was becoming very distressed about making choices and decisions; there were too many. So we worked with him to narrow down his choices, so that later we can open them back up again when he can cope with them. We managed his diary, an open diary was too much for him.

One boy only wanted to play with water, so the staff started reducing the time when the water tray was set out in the wing. Now, he can still enjoy the water, but he has learnt to enjoy doing other things, to contain the water within the water tray, and to contain what he does with it. We decided not to use water as a reward for him or for any of the children with challenging behaviour, because you should have access to water on principle, and not only as a reward. Another child loves going to the early years wing and we did discuss whether that should be a reward but we decided that he should have access to that as a matter of course, and his rewards could be adult contact or to choose who went with him to early years.

One child became obsessed with pencils, and that is managed in the same way as with the water – though it's slightly harder when there are so many pencils around. But the staff and children have become much more thoughtful about where they put them. This boy is also interested in controlling his pencil drawings, and making shapes and patterns. The staff are very clear, 'Now you can have your pencil, now it's finished and we'll move on to the next thing.' And they use all kinds of techniques like photographs and symbols. The curriculum is dynamic enough to help all the children to become interested in a broader range of objects and activities.

We agree that children whose behaviour could be described as autistic need secure routines, and we consider that the structure in each wing is very consistent and probably tighter than in many primary schools. The staff work hard to ensure that they are all consistent, and the team teaching helps here. All children need to know their boundaries and to know that each member of staff, within reason, will say pretty much the same thing about what they can do. Yet it is a question of balance. If the curriculum is too restricted and the school days too repetitive, that can reinforce the tendency of some children to follow unnecessary rituals. It can also make it harder for them to become interested in other things, if there is not enough variety and stimulation. We find that these children learn and progress, within the balance between over- and under stimulation which we are always working to achieve. They also benefit from being friends and being equals with all the other children here.

This school could be quite difficult to work in because there are quite challenging children. But because everyone believes in negotiation, inclusion, flexibility, support, enabling, the outcome is that all children benefit from the experience. There isn't that much racial tension or sexism here. Inclusion has ripples for everybody. Certainly, professionally, the staff's careers are enhanced by working here because of this experience, and everyone has gone on to promoted posts. It is good that they move on to spread ideas about inclusion, although sometimes they find it is hard to interest staff in other schools. It is easier in a school that believes in the child's rights through the general principle of inclusion.

Relationships

In 1992, we had a term to prepare before the school opened, and at first we didn't do much about inclusion. We thought about what our school was going to look like. We had a training weekend and did lots of work about personal development and self-awareness, and what knowledge we share or do not share with others, and how that affects working relationships. We talked about how we would work together, and therefore how we would work with the children, as a team-based school. We set the aims and objectives during that summer term, a core group of staff set up the school, and we had a week's training session in September to plan the curriculum – you had to have your ethos before you could have your curriculum, without that culture you can't do the rest. That is particularly important when you start from the notion of including every child and every parent who arrives here. So we had to think about ourselves as human beings before we could think about what we were going to do with other human beings. The aims and objectives haven't changed much, although we review them annually and we change the language a little.

Rules follow from relationships and they are about enabling people to work together and decide what is an acceptable morality. The way people are outraged when codes are broken suggests we have quite high morality here. The jewelled cat stickers that are used to reward the children are left out on a basket in a hallway, and hardly anyone ever takes an extra one. If anyone does, the other children quickly notice and protest.

The children understand that if they behave badly, they will be told off by the staff working with them, and if the behaviour persists they will end up with seeing Brigid and privileges will be withdrawn. Discipline is intended to enable them to work together to develop self-discipline and have a nice time, and to know that if they break a basic tenet they don't have a nice time. Discipline is also about learning how to work in the world. Children have quite a hard time with the rules of their family, the rules of society, and the rules of the school, three sets of rules. Schools have to enable them to deal with those three sets, and to perceive adults as supporters and enablers, not as people who come down heavy-handedly.

Children develop their own self-morality – such as that it is wrong to hit someone else – and they have to learn to manage their own behaviour and their temper. Positivity as the other side of negativity is a useful notion – realising that they have a better time if they like people and get on well with them and avoid conflict. They also need to know that the head teacher will impose discipline when necessary.

Children have the right to feel jealous or angry, to feel that other people get on their nerves, or to be unhappy or disappointed. But they don't have the right to make some one else feel like that. And the school should help them to be able to say, 'Okay I'm jealous that someone else is doing what I want to do, but maybe I'll be able to do that tomorrow.' The staff will say to children, 'I understand that you are upset, or why you are angry, however, hitting them back doesn't help.' You have to do a lot of work with the children and some parents about hitting back, and say, 'At what point does it stop?' Children have to learn to trust adults to sort it out for them.

In deciding rules, we look at what enables good behaviour in the school. Essentially, you don't need lots of rules such as, 'Don't run in the corridor', because those are outcomes of behaviour. The principles of behaviour are to treat people properly, respect them and care for them and for the equipment. We emphasise a positive approach to relationships between human beings and with the environment, so in a sense there are very few rules.

At the beginning of each year, the staff teams decide the

behaviour they can expect in the wing so that all staff are consistent, which is very important. They have to reach a reasonable agreement on how formal or informal they think the standards of behaviour should be. The staff also have to agree on a shared level of school expectations, such as not running in the corridor because someone could get knocked over.

The more rules you have, the more challenges and conflicts you can set up. Discipline has to be about how you treat other human beings. If a teacher tells you to do something, as a child you should do it. If you have a difficulty about that, you have the right to talk about it. You shouldn't simply refuse, or have a temper tantrum, because that goes against the rules of the world. But we make space to negotiate. We hope that all the time the staff are fairly reasonable, and listen and if it is possible are willing to change things, with flexibility within a structure.

We encourage the children to talk about rules and to choose the main rules for their wing.

Early years wing

- be happy
- be friends
- tidy up when you finish
- look after the books
- don't throw things.

Key stage 2A

- respect and care for ourselves and each other
- look after the equipment and keep the wing tidy
- talk quietly and be polite
- walk sensibly in the wing
- work hard and learn.

Discipline and sanctions

We don't often use the word punish, we try to use the language of what is acceptable or unacceptable and to enable children to work it out for themselves: How would you feel if . . . ? What would happen if . . . ? There are privileges in the school such as going to the park, the soft play room or the ball pool, which are withdrawn as a punishment, or they do dinner duty. Some children do that for pleasure and they get jewelled cats, and others do it as a punishment and do not get a reward. We work much more with rewards and celebrating achievement than with punishments. Older children have certificates, and when they have five of these they have a book token.

Sometimes children say that 'special needs children hit us and don't get told off'. One child would bite people. We explain that she uses different ways to communicate with you, she doesn't use words, she uses gestures. When she gets frustrated she uses biting whereas you (the other children) have lots of ways of sharing your feelings, you can talk to people and do all sorts of things. As adults we understand it is difficult, but you can't repeat that behaviour because you know it's wrong to do that. So we work on this notion that some people have limited approaches. The children have to learn that one reason she bites is when they invade her space, and they have to try to avoid doing this. It's hard for children on a rollator to play football, and therefore sometimes you should allow for this by passing them the ball.

A child with special needs who has negative behaviour will be told off with the same principle as all the children. We are always working towards the time when the child will not do that. You might not be able to discuss it much with them in long sentences, and that might seem like a double standard to the children who would be told off in more detail. Basically you just say, 'No, stop,' without going into all the 'how would you feel if it happened to you?' and talking, perhaps, for 15 minutes.

Rules or virtues

When the writing committee talked about rules for this chapter, they kept moving away from rules to talk about responsibilities and moral feelings.

Delicia: And there was some bullying then with the Year 6s who have left now and that wasn't very nice, and this year it's been much better.

Patrick: Some people didn't take no notice, but it has been better this year. Our year get on better together.

Delicia: Yes and we're nicer to the little ones.

Sarah: For a reward you can go to Brigid and get a jewelled cat, they're shiny sticker things all different shapes. Patrick's got a book full of them. You can choose them. Some children give them to each other, my friend got a jewelled cat and she gave it to me.

(We talk about friends and forgiving or not feeling able to forgive.)

Priscilla: We're not getting very far on these rules. Do you think on the whole it is fairly good here and you just do the best you can?

Sarah: Yes, we don't have much arguing now.

Delicia: Yes, we don't think of rules really, we just have our own rules. We will do our best, that is one rule we will do.

Priscilla: Only you can decide that, no one can force you to?

Delicia: If you want to do your best, you do your best.

Sarah: But if someone's really bad, they go to Brigid and this year I don't think no one's gone to Brigid, not for a really bad fight.

Delicia: No. But in the early years, they're training for their rules for when they grow up to Key Stage 1. They take the register to Brigid so it learns them so the teachers can trust those children. Say I didn't trust Sarah, I couldn't say to her 'Sarah look after my money', but I could always trust a teacher. The teachers in our school are like Samaritans, we had Samaritans round our school and we had a video about them.

Sarah: My friend told me loads of secrets but I don't tell other people. I trust her.

Delicia: Me and Sarah are best friends we trust each other, we work together and everything.

A parent

Jesus commanded us to love God with your whole heart and to love your neighbour as yourself. The school seems to have this rule that anything against anyone else is a major rule. The rule is to be kind to each other, to think of others. If everybody in the world obeyed that law, we wouldn't have the problems in the world we do. So maybe that's another reason in general, though you're always going to get isolated cases against it, that in general when you come into the school it is quite good, and the children know what behaviour will be tolerated. If my son is punched or scratched, a form is filled out, the staff take great care, they tell you whether they spoke to the other child, that kind of thing. Obviously they have certain rules and routines the children stick to, I can't say any ones in particular, but the main rule is being well mannered and polite to each other, and especially where the special needs children are concerned they're very – they really try to help. If everybody really did behave like this, there would not need to be rules because, then, everything else automatically follows, I suppose, everything else will fall into place.

This staff could say to children, 'That's naughty', but they say, 'No it's not fair to the other children', and they show the children to be fair. So it still keeps coming into this loving way about it. I do like that because that's what I try to uphold in my family and that's an extension of that here.

Chapter 5
Fun

Like the themes of other chapters, such as community and equality, fun relates to many aspects of the school and weaves through the other chapters. There is no English word for the broad mixture of things that are interesting, satisfying, amusing, rewarding, maybe exciting, challenging or difficult, and are enjoyable and worthwhile in themselves, for their own sake, as well as being useful for extra purposes such as gaining skill and knowledge. We use 'fun' to mean all these things. This chapter looks at the enjoyable aspects of everyday school life: learning and teaching, drama, assemblies, dinner time, encouraging high self-esteem and inter-dependency, making decisions, and the extra fun activities.

Learning and teaching

Learning should be fun. There is some strange idea that it should be boring and dull and that somehow children have to be made to learn. But learning is a natural thing we do as human beings, through play and finding out. The difficulty with twentieth century learning is the idea that you go to a different place to do learning, with strict rules and certain things you have to learn, in a certain way, with a certain higher order of skills. This doesn't take into account learning through play.

Our whole school is based on the principles of the early years approach, which are about self-motivation, fostering self-esteem and learning through doing – the experiential approach. The idea is to continue with the enjoyment young children have in learning which is fun and interesting, learning through play and through making mistakes. The approach also emphasises group activities rather than whole-class teaching.

Enjoyment is an essential part of good teaching and learning relationships.

Ashir, Zak, Azizuh, Maroah and Beatrice described a good teacher as some one who:

- really listens and understands you;
- sorts things out straight away;
- doesn't stand for attitude or bullying or abuse;
- is fair in telling off any child, is not more strict with some than with others;
- supports and helps you with your work;
- doesn't just say, 'Look it up in the dictionary' if you can't spell a word, but tells you the first few letters so that you can look it up;
- says things like 'do you mind getting me a rubber, please?'
- gives you a cup of tea in the staff room;
- if we win a football match, takes us to McDonald's;
- if you have a problem says, 'Come and sit down and talk about it and we'll sort it out', not just 'Go and talk to your Mum'.

If you feel close to a teacher you can talk to them, and if you're not keen on a teacher in your wing, you can choose another one.

Cleves' OFSTED Report (1998) stated:

Teachers, support staff and adult volunteers have very good working relationships. These help to create an atmosphere where pupils' well-being can be nurtured and supported positively. The staff provide a safe environment in which the pupils can feel secure ... [and] comfortable about taking the risk of learning from their mistakes. This is having a positive effect on the standards they achieve.

Drama

Shea (freelance drama teacher in several schools)

Cleves has a fairly enlightened curriculum. A lot of good things in primary schools are beginning to disappear, like the play corner in reception classes, but if the arts generally are downgraded, how can children have a broad and balanced education? Of course, literacy and maths are important, but in many schools there is no drama at all. Most people, including those in OFSTED and QCA [Qualifications and Curriculum Authority] recognise drama as a powerful way of learning. It helps personal development including self-confidence, taking turns, taking risks in a safe way because fiction, make believe, provides a safety net. It extends and enriches the child's whole cultural experience.

Fiction can bring in all kinds of people, lifestyles, situations, issues, concepts, events, stories and ideas, and through drama we work on them and explore them. Drama provides experiences that school, as real life, cannot easily provide. Drama is an important form of literacy, and multiple sign system. If they want to know, for example, what adults are thinking, children depend on gesture, intonation and expressions, on reading all kinds of cues from people in action. Drama involves a dual process when children are active story makers and co-authors making decisions about what will happen, and they also experience the events of the drama as the people in the story. They are holding two worlds in their minds at the same time when they are in the classroom and pretending that they are in a castle and are conscious of both: I am making it happen, and it is happening to me. Children say to me, 'Is it real?' In a way, they have to be conscious that it is not real while being deeply absorbed, for example, when we do Hansel and Gretel I can be a really scary witch. With drama you have the freedom to make another ending, to act a story one way and then change the story and that can be a good way of learning. One time Mr Misery is pleased when his house is cleaned and another time he remains miserable.

This school sees drama as a means of learning and an art form, so the children have opportunities for dramatic play, and structured teacher-led drama, and regular performances such as school plays, and work that grows from and is shaped by their other curriculum work. Drama goes on all the time – school plays, dance, assemblies, telling stories, television, film, it's part of the culture. At this school I tend to have to get them into role more quickly, with less talking beforehand about what we're going to do, but these children tend to give more ideas along the way, such as about what could happen next. I get children to demonstrate more to each other here, they are keen and confident to do that. Drama is a form of literacy that they can achieve success and satisfaction with, and quite often they are motivated then to transfer their stories into writing.

Last year's Year 6 worked in three groups, and one group did hopes and fears about going to secondary school. We talked about these and acted them out, nightmare scenarios, like not having any friends, getting lost, being bullied, not being able to find their way home. It was quite real although we laughed a lot as well. Hopes were a reversal of fears on the whole. We cast ourselves, usually the best person to do a part was the one who had the first idea. We did chorus work as a rap written by one of the children which they all learnt and we combined different sorts of drama, still pictures, flashback, bad dreams, playing scenes one way then another. For example, with bullying, What might happen? How would it start? Then we would play it again. What do we do? What's the worst thing that could happen? What do we do now? We put all the parts together and acted them for all the Years 5 and 6. It was important that they felt comfortable and confident about performing in front of other people. They had just come back from staying on the barge which seemed to have made them much more confident.

Another group did Macbeth, mainly the first half of the play up to killing the King. At first they read in turns, eight people would all read parts of one speech, then they memorised some speeches, and in the end there was one person for each part. They improvised some sections between the longer speeches. It was quite easy for them to enjoy Shakespeare's text, you can make it immediate and clear for them. They were acting, shouting and pointing. 'Fie on thee!' is a fine thing to say, they understood it very quickly. They're used to naturalistic acting from television so I had to get them to over-act at times as in a theatre. The rest of the wing seemed to enjoy watching it and that also provides a model for future work. This year's Year 6 who watched Macbeth have asked if they can do a play too like that.

About five children found the other groups boring, so we made up a play through my asking them questions. They did the work and wanted to perform it. They worked out the events, the characters, the staging and props, whether they wanted props and how to use them, with a lot of attention to detail. The play was about going to an old house and falling into a secret tunnel and meeting zombies, the undead, and somehow making their escape. They moved on from playing at ghosts to more serious acting and polishing their work for a performance without my needing to tell them to do this. They were able to work very independently, whereas the other two groups needed more help from me to structure the first play and to share in working on the Shakespearian play.

Assembly

Every Friday we celebrate everyone in the school from three-year-olds to the adults. Assembly lasts about 30 minutes. We start by having music, like the Beatle's *All You Need is Love*, or R. Kelly's *I Believe I could Fly, I Believe I could Touch the Sky*, or The Christians' *Harvest for the World*. People come into the hall in groups chatting. Some children walk slowly supported by the staff, some of the younger disabled ones are carried in, some children push others in wheelchairs. We sit on the floor and some of us clap to the music. As usual, people are wearing many kinds of clothes and colours – jeans or shorts or tracksuits, long or short skirts, lacy dresses, or headscarves.

Then we start with a song that says 'hello' in several languages, followed by a 'how do you do?' song when we all shake hands. We clap ourselves after every song. The children whose birthday it is this week go to stand at the front beside the candles and we sing 'happy birthday', lots of people sign the words as they sing. Each birthday child chooses in turn for us to give them three claps or blow three kisses. Then we have more applause for people who have worked hard this week. We sing more songs like *Love is Something if You Give it Away*, or *Catch Me the Colours of the Rainbow*. If the singing and clapping get very noisy and excited, then we whisper a verse. The choir might sing, or the brass or recorder group will play some music and, after we have clapped them, Brigid says, for example, 'Now quietly close your eyes. We have just sung about how if you give love away you get more love back. Think about who you are going to give your love to this weekend.' After a short silence we might sing *Shalom* very softly. Brigid will talk about some good news and say we have all done very well and deserve another clap. We sing a goodbye song in several languages and then Brigid turns up loud music, which we sing and clap to, while groups leave the hall in turn. The early years children go first and they wave to their friends in the other years.

A parent

> The assembly is like one big family. I think the thing I was most impressed about was when I sat in an assembly once and Brigid said, 'Close your eyes', and I must admit I thought 'Oh no' because of my own beliefs. But it wasn't like a prayer, all she did was say, 'Everybody grab somebody else's hand', everybody was sitting on the floor, and she said, 'Close your eyes. Think about something that you did good this week for somebody.' I felt very moved, the way she said that, and she said, 'Then try and do

something nice over the weekend. Now open your eyes, I think you should all give yourselves a clap.' I think that really is an experience that sums up the whole school, they have this family bond, and they commend the children when they do something nice for someone else, and for their parents, and the teachers encourage them and listen to them when they talk about their parents. It is very unique for a school, that family bond. Maybe the open plan does contribute to the family atmosphere.

Extract from OFSTED Report

[The pupils] have considerable respect for and awareness of other people's feelings and beliefs. The daily act of collective worship [in each wing] is of good quality. Each week there is a special assembly to celebrate achievement and important events. This is a 'wonder-full' occasion. It is filled with joy and praise as pupils share their talents and successes and give thanks as a happy caring community. Moral development is very good. It is promoted consistently so that pupils understand the need to trust and be trusted. The school teaches the difference between right and wrong in all contexts of daily life as part of the learning process. All the staff work hard to help pupils to understand the importance of taking responsibility for their actions and understanding the consequences of their behaviour towards each other.

The provision for social development is very good. It reflects the positive strong ethos of this school as a provider of inclusive education... Work in art and music complements and celebrates the rich cultural diversity of the school's staff and pupils as well as the western cultural tradition.

Enjoying school as a community

At lunch time, we clear up and then sit in base groups talking or reading. Then some wings go out to play, while for the ones who go first for their lunch a child arrives every few minutes to call a few more ones to queue in the dining hall. We collect our trays, and we can take time to choose what food we want. Then we look for a spare place where someone who has come in earlier has finished. We have to carry the trays carefully through the narrow spaces because the dining room is small and crowded. The staff help some children to eat their lunch. There are roughly three sittings, but people are coming in and going out nearly all the time. The staff make sure that we are all right and that the tables are wiped, but they don't usually have to tell us what to do.

A teacher

The school policy is that dinner time is a social occasion, a chance for children and adults to sit, relax and talk together. Visitors, including parents, are encouraged to have lunch, and sometimes parents are sent invitations to lunch when there is a celebration. We avoid having long queues and mass movements around the school because those are times when bullying and disruption are most likely to happen. Instead of the staff spending time on trying to manage and control behaviour, we spend time here on planning the curriculum and the use of resources, and on ways of preventing disruption and avoiding routines which could encourage it, and that is very important.

The aims in our school documents (see Appendix 1 for examples) show how every day we want to celebrate achievements, and to set high expectations for realising our potential and feeling that the sky is the limit. We emphasise interdependency, rather than competition, to help people to feel confident. We learn to enjoy making decisions with the risk of making mistakes, and the challenge of learning from them.

A teacher

> Self-esteem and interdependency go together, when you respect yourself and everyone else. We have learnt so much from being with the children with profound difficulties. For example, in the playground, the larger children rush around past the small frail ones and although they look casual they are careful not to knock into them. Different games and groups play happily alongside each other, somehow managing not to spoil each other's play. If you look round the playground and the park play area when we go there, you hardly ever see a child playing alone, they are all in pairs and groups. The staff on duty keep making sure that the children are considerate, and avoid conflict and respect each other's space. We encourage them to learn and play in gender and ability and age mixed groups. When children play on their own, we watch to see that they seem happy and not isolated.

A parent

> At playtimes you see them pushing the wheelchairs. They don't patronise the special needs children or go 'Aah' as if they are different. They're caring and they're extra loving but not to a degree where they pamper them or make them seem like there's something wrong with them. I don't know if the teachers specifically say something to the children, or that they show by example, I suppose that's what they follow, as a kind of rule – that they are to help them, but not treat them as babies.

We enjoy creative work, for example, when we think, write and talk about many things, from our own identity to the world around us, as shown in these poems.

I'm Black, by Ayan

> I am black: I love my colour
> I wouldn't change for other colours.
>
> But some people call black people this black sheep, black dirt, but think for one moment and think if that was you . . . !
>
> Say to yourself that I will never do that again. Let's live in peace in this world for ever, Our peoples.

Peace on earth, by Fadumo

All these bright and beautiful things will soon die away . . .
So why wait?
Why not let there be peace on earth?
Why not work together in peace and harmony?
You think there's time to have your fun by making people sad and miserable, lonely and afraid, making them feel they don't belong on earth.
Why wait?
Peace rules!

Sharing decisions

Everyone from the youngest child is encouraged to enjoy having a part in making decisions and planning their day.

Joy

There are lots of different early years approaches. With some, everything is labelled and accessible, and children take out what they want to do, go ahead with doing it, and at the end they have the responsibility for putting it away. So you don't arrange the activities and the tables and make it look beautiful, like we do here.

I feel we've got the best of both worlds, because I do want them to feel, 'Oh, wow, wonderful', when they come in. I do want it to be set up for the teachers to use their flair and artistic ability and stimulate children, and give a message to parents that we really care about their children by setting it up so beautifully. But if a child ever wants to follow another pattern, or get out another drawer, fine. If it's something big, like they say to me, 'Oh, you haven't got the train set out, Joy', and it takes ages to set it up, I'll say, 'We'll get it out this afternoon' and we can negotiate. They'll not be complaining, just saying they really enjoy playing with it.

With, say, the big bricks, we might think of a prompt to develop their play. OFSTED said they are really pleased about the role play that is going on. We might build dens outside, and the teachers get involved, without being over the top, and heavy, and making every single thing a learning opportunity. We have to know when the key learning moments are, and then leave it. But there are other times when you can interrupt exciting play and the children will be a bit disturbed if you intervene at the wrong moment. I think it's having the knowledge and experience and confidence to stand back. And all the time we encourage them to organise their day.

Fun times and places

The writing committee talked a lot about things we enjoy, and here are some examples.

We've got several fun places. There's the hall where we have music, drama and dancing and PE and assemblies and school concerts. There's the soft play room, and the ball pool in the foyer, we all like using that sometimes. We've got a sensory room with big clear plastic tubes and you press a knob and watch the bubbles rise up through them and the coloured lights. You can make clouds move across the ceiling and play different kinds of music, and it makes you relax and feel calm. These places have a list of 'dos and don'ts' like 'take off your shoes' and the last 'do' is 'remember to have fun and enjoy your session!' The park is next to the school and sometimes we do PE there on the swings and climbing frames. It's nice going there with all your friends.

Our wing has its own garden. We're making a pond and we grow herbs and vegetables and flowers in the garden, about seven of us are doing it with Jim, our teacher. We've dug the hole. We hope it is done before we leave at the end of term, but anyway we'll come back here to see it. We want to make our wing's garden nice because at the moment there's quite a lot of weeds. We have a team working on it and we bring plants and seeds. We are going to have a fence round the pond to stop the children jumping into it.

We played trust games. Simone [teacher] put some ropes up high in our playground and we had to work as a team of about 30, our base group, to see how we could all get over the ropes without touching them. We done it as a whole class. It took us a while to see how to do it, and we found we could all help each other over, except for the last person who was left behind. Afterwards Simone told us how another group had solved it so that they could all get over the ropes. We had to learn to cooperate, and we do that in PE when we all have to do something together. Sometimes we write stories in groups.

We go to stay on a barge in Essex, and we can go swimming and do lots of things. I wish we could stay there longer. Last time, Carol came with us and she took us on a night walk and we saw all the lights from the ships. We went on another night walk such a long way we had to get the minibus back. And some people told spooky stories in the dark. On one night walk you follow ropes wound round among the trees feeling your way in the dark. One group went to France for three days.

We have lots of novels and a library in our wing, and we can take books home if we take the tag out of the book and leave it here. We can bring in special books of our own.

Every summer time we do a big spring cleaning, we clean our school and throw away the rubbish we don't want no more, at the end of the year.

We've got a forest room in our wing in a little central room. (The other little room like this is the office for the teachers. If we go and work in there on the computer we're not allowed to mess it up.) The forest room was set up as a surprise for us. For two weeks we were not allowed to go in. Simone put curtains up, and it was really good when she done it all. The collages are of the forest and Simone done it all branches on the ceiling, green and blue walls, ivy and little trees, palm trees and jungle animals and a snake. Michael brought his lizard in a cage to school. Our goldfish died so Simone got a toy parrot for us. There's toy animals on the branches of some trees in here. When we went to Waltham Abbey we found a big log in the lake and we lifted it out. We were allowed to take it home on the coach and it really stank. We cleaned it and now it is in the forest. This room is used for all sorts of things. Three ladies come in and help some of us with reading and writing. [They are staff from National Westminster Bank who are part of the Newham Business Partnership Green Court Project. They initially came for six weeks, but have now been coming for six months and each person hears three children read.]

We wrote a poem as a group, about babyhood, we was all thinking about it and Sarah wrote it down and now she's writing it on the computer and we might read it out in Assembly.

The small room in Key Stage 1 wing

We would like to have more time to talk to our friends. The only break is at lunch time from 12 to 1, and then you might be asked to do things, or if you want to play football or basketball then you can't talk to your friends then, of course. And we'd like more time to do our garden as well. There isn't enough time to do all the things we like doing here.

Chapter 6
The Cleves School experience: conclusion

Meeting challenges

We began this book by pointing out potential contradictions between trying to achieve high test results and include children of all abilities, between the crowded academic curriculum and due attention to creativity and fun, between expecting children to be well-disciplined and also able to think critically and independently, between having a strong corporate identity in a school and welcoming newcomers and visitors, while respecting difference and diversity. Through the book we have described the ways we try to resolve these tensions and do justice to all these aims.

Repeatedly, we find that ways we develop of helping one group of children or promoting one aim in the school benefit other children and aims. Through including children with profound difficulties we have learned how to develop a much wider range of learning activities and to be aware of children's differing needs at all the ability levels. As the mixed ability teaching and learning methods have improved, our national curriculum test levels have also improved, especially the value added results, showing how the children progress while they are at the school.

The team teaching enables each child to benefit from the expertise, preparation work and teaching skills of six teachers through the day as well as help from the learning support staff. The teachers benefit from being able to specialise instead of having to prepare and teach across the whole curriculum for one class. Team teaching enables us to cover a wide curriculum and also to enjoy music and art, sports and many other activities. These help the children to enjoy being at school and with one another and to be enthusiastic and well motivated.

The teachers' examples of sharing and cooperation through team teaching encourage the children to share and cooperate, to be kind and helpful, without being forced or criticised, because, it seems, they want to behave well and they find this rewarding.

Team teaching involves the staff knowing each child well but not having to be so close that difficulties between them become stressful for either person. The children learn to work independently and also cooperatively. The team teachers find the work tiring and demanding but less stressful and more interesting than when they worked as individual class teachers. The confidence they gain through working in teams encourages them to welcome and exchange challenging new ideas. They welcome visitors and new staff and children, respecting their differences, as the children also tend to do confidently.

The school is constantly changing, partly as education policies change. As a resourced school, when some of the special schools were being closed, we admitted numbers of children with severe or profound difficulties. So, as some of our disabled children come from outside our catchment area, Cleves is not a typical school of the kind that will evolve when every child can attend the nearest primary school as schools become more inclusive. We agree with this policy which will take time to achieve and we are at a stage towards that time. Yet we expect there will always be a place for resourced schools which take higher numbers of children with certain disabilities such as children with a hearing impairment. Then they can belong to their own group, as well as to other groups and to the wider community in the school.

Two main things can exclude people – the curriculum and buildings. Schools have to develop flexible policies which enable every child to have access to the curriculum through differentiated teaching and also physical access through the building. This may be easy to arrange, like having a little extra supervision in corridors and stairways when children move around the school, and this can benefit every child in the school. The important issue is not, for example, stairs as a potential barrier, but what you do about the stairs. Old buildings can be used imaginatively. For example in the old three-decker Victorian schools you could have the youngest children on the top floor, because it is easier to carry them up there until lifts are installed. Team teaching and using a set of classrooms instead of having each class in separate rooms can be arranged in many schools, with central shared areas and the classrooms around them. You can put in worktop shelves and carpets, and then you are able to get rid of many chairs and tables to have more space for equipment and activities, space to move freely between activities and for access for children who use wheelchairs. The teachers of each Key Stage can work as a team with added support staff and nursery nurses. Working fully in a team doesn't include staff going into their own room and closing the door, but it means sharing everything with a whole team.

The basic difference that makes a school inclusive is not the building or resources but the attitudes. We hope that this book will be useful to other schools who are developing ways of working more inclusively.

Appendix 1
Implementing the aims of Cleves School

Cleves School documents

The documents at Cleves concentrate on the climate that the children work in, before going on to the content of the work. We used the Newham LEA format then added our ideas. We don't have a separate document on equal opportunities because they are referred to through all the documents and relate to everything. In Newham schools, special needs are seen as an equal opportunities issue, along with race and gender, but the Government requires every school to have a special needs policy document so we do have one. Our policy documents describe and explain what we do, and are led by the actual practice. The Schemes of Work documents are about the details of what we do. They recognise the differentiated curriculum, so you might have activities that are relevant for Year 3 and also some that are relevant for the early years, because there are children who need those activities. It was quite complex to start off with, to work out how to do that! As an example of one of our documents, we include a section from the one on our aims. The summary was quoted in Chapter 1.

Aim

To develop high positive self-esteem in all children and adults.

Implementation

Adults

- The work of everyone is valued and displayed around the school. A variety of languages, including Makaton, is used to explain the displays.
- Children are made aware of their strengths and weaknesses, how to celebrate their strengths and improve their weaknesses through discussion with adults and members of their peer group.
- We have a marking policy that ensures children feel good about their work and which enables them to move forward.

- We praise children and discuss their needs constructively.
- We plan a rich curriculum that counteracts and challenges negative stereotypes.
- Records of achievement show children how well they are achieving and heighten their pride in themselves and their work.
- We enable children to express their views and opinions appropriately and with confidence.
- At all times we are polite and caring to all children and adults and show them respect.
- At all times, we present positive images of ourselves and the children.

Children

- are enabled to express their views and opinions appropriately and with confidence;
- are made aware of their strengths and weaknesses, how to celebrate their strengths and improve their weaknesses through discussion with adults and members of their peer group;
- are enabled to feel confident about attempting a task by being provided with a supportive environment;
- are aware that making mistakes is part of learning;
- are supported in working collaboratively and cooperatively through shared tasks and outcomes;
- take responsibility for their environment;
- adults set ground rules together and are aware of boundaries;
- are made aware of the way teachers relate to them, e.g. through direction and the use of negotiation;
- celebrate the diversity of cultures, languages and life experiences of the families in the school through the curriculum, resources and organisation;
- successfully gain new knowledge, skills and concepts and have a great sense of pride in their achievement;
- are made aware that they have rights and that these rights are adhered to both in school and in their life out of school.

Aim   To enable children to be aware of their interdependency on each other.

Principles

- We all need to learn to give and accept support.
- It is important to develop knowledge and understanding of other people, cultures, classes, religions and learning needs.
- Everyone is active in the learning process.
- All children are decision-makers.
- Working together collaboratively leads to success.
- Interdependency creates a sense of belonging and lessens selfishness and insecurity.

Implementation

children can demonstrate understanding of, and the benefits of, interdependency through:

- sharing of tasks, ideas, skills and resources as well as discussion about the benefits of interdependency;
- tasks which require collaboration;
- a variety of group sizes and both genders working together;
- targeting of specific skills in curriculum planning, e.g. listening–sharing–cooperation;
- individuals not dominating class time or space – turn-taking as an intrinsic part of group practice;
- all children being included in groupings;
- using a range of communication skills including Makaton and British Sign Language;
- whole-school celebrations involving everyone, including parents;
- the use of team games to demonstrate, explicitly, the need to work together;
- careful choice of games and activities to engender their sense of being supported, e.g. parachute games;
- children having a sense of belonging to the school community and feeling safe and secure in school.

Aim

To acknowledge that all children are decision-makers and to enable them to become active participants in their own learning.

Principles

- Children learn best when they are enabled to be decision-makers and trusted to play a central role in their own learning.
- All children have the right to take part in the decision-making process that affects them.
- Adult/child relationships are enhanced when children are aware that they are active participants in their learning.

Implementation

- Children are aware of what resources are available and where they are located, what the resources are for and how to use them.
- Teachers and other adults are aware of when and how to intervene to support children's learning, assessing when to intervene is part of our ongoing in-service programme.
- Our learning environment enables children to make decisions; children are set open-ended tasks to facilitate this decision-making process.
- Children are given the opportunities and skills to reflect on the outcomes of decisions they have made.

- Children are enabled to understand the restraints of time and funding when making decisions.
- Adults act as role models in decision-making to help children to feel confident about making and taking decisions.

All the other aims are considered in similar detail in the full document.

Appendix 2
Extracts from the 1998 OFSTED Report

In all wings, adults provide pupils with good examples of co-operative and caring behaviour. The staff work together to create a warm but disciplined atmosphere.

The school's work is enriched by links with the local community [and these] make a strong contribution to the effective life of the school.

Staff governors and parents share the common goals of developing positive relationships and providing a curriculum that encourages self-respect, that values the individual and promotes achievement.

The school aims to provide an environment where each child of every race, gender, class and learning need is truly recognised, accepted and valued, where there is a feeling of belonging in which all can develop high and positive self-esteem. It aims to help children develop a sense of interdependence and to ensure that the whole-school community works together to enable children to access the whole curriculum and to reach their potential.

Spiritual, moral, social and cultural development

Spiritual development is fostered effectively through planned themes for assemblies and worship. The themes are developed in circle time and in religious education and also feature in the wider curriculum. For example, pupils in the reception class discussed the story of the Chinese New Year and considered how the animals reacted to God's suggestion for resolving their problem. The themes of forgiveness and self-belief are explored, by pupils in several classes, in singing, listening to and appraising performance in music. Older pupils can talk confidently about their own beliefs. They have considerable respect for and awareness of other people's feelings and beliefs. The school teaches the difference between right and wrong in all contexts of daily life as part of the learning process.

Moral development is very good. Pupils understand the need to trust and to be trusted. All staff work hard to help pupils understand the importance of taking responsibility for their actions and understanding the consequences of their behaviour towards each other.

The provision for social development is excellent. It reflects in a positive and strong way the ethos of this school as a provider of inclusive education. Pupils support each other throughout the day without being prompted. Adults in the school provide excellent role models in their relationships with pupils and with each other. Older pupils are encouraged to look after younger pupils at lunch-time as well as supporting their friends who may have disabilities. The school provides a range of extra-curricular activities which are mainly sports orientated and pupils are very proud to be chosen to represent the school. There are opportunities for pupils to participate in a range of musical activities. They sing in the choir and learn to play musical instruments. Cultural development is good. It complements and celebrates the rich cultural diversity of the school's staff and pupils. The school has established links with support groups in the community and encourages visitors to talk to the pupils about their experiences at home and abroad. Fabrics from many parts of the world are used as a stimulus for observational drawing and collage work. Displays celebrate a range of festivals such as Diwali and the Chinese New Year.

One of the great strengths of the school is the very high quality of relationships within it. These are based on mutual respect, trust, affection, concern and sensitivity to people's needs and feelings. The degree of racial harmony is excellent. Pupils accept the wide range of attitudes, beliefs, backgrounds, abilities and needs as a natural part of the school's lively and enriching environment. They value each other as people, regardless of individual circumstances and needs. For example, there was genuine pleasure taken by pupils in the contribution of a child with physical disabilities in a drama lesson.

Throughout the school the pupils with special educational needs receive a high degree of support and make satisfactory progress overall and in relation to the targets set on their individual education plans. The pupils who speak English as an additional language receive good specialist support. The special feature of the school is its inclusive approach and this has a profound effect on developing pupils' acceptance and tolerance of others with different abilities and disabilities.

Attitudes, behaviour and personal development

Pupils in all age groups have very positive attitudes to school. They like to be given good opportunities to learn new things. They respond well to what they are asked to do, especially where the work matches closely their skills and needs. For instance, in the nursery and reception classes they are very enthusiastic about creative work. At the beginning of Key Stage 2, pupils thrive on the challenge of working out, in maths lessons, how and why they arrive at a particular answer. In Key Stage 1, pupils have regular opportunities to make choices and show initiative in their daily diaries. In these, pupils record the order in which they will do some of their work.

The personal and social development of the three- and four-year-olds is good. They respond well to the very positive encouragement and example of the adults who work with them. All are keen to learn new words and to use 'signing' so that they can join in all the social activities, including singing together. Pupils behave well in and around the school. They want to please adults by responding well to the positive example set by all the staff. They cooperate with adults in all settings. It is very unusual for the particularly challenging behaviour of a child with special educational needs to disrupt other pupils. Invariably such behaviour is managed well by staff. Pupils take care of each other very well, with a very high level of kindness and sensitivity. Pupils with disabilities respond with pleasure to the efforts made by the other pupils to include them in their games and work groups.

There are many examples of pupils stepping in to stop arguments or to include someone standing outside a group in a game, as well as telling a teacher when a child is unhappy or has fallen over. When incidents of bullying occur, they are dealt with effectively. The school has not excluded any pupils in the past year and has only ever excluded one child.

All the disabled children enjoy the park

Attendance

Attendance is satisfactory. The pupils include some whose special educational needs and health involve inevitable periods of absence, some of which are long. This makes it more difficult for the school to achieve high attendance levels overall. However, the school manages to reach and sometimes exceed 90% attendance, term by term. Pupils are very keen to come to school and do not stay away without good reason. Very few pupils arrive late. There is no disruption to lessons because of lack of punctuality.

The school has very good systems in place to promote discipline and good behaviour. Pupils who have difficulty behaving appropriately are given clear, consistent and constructive help in getting on with other people and coping with simple classroom rules. The systems to deal with bullying are good. They start by ensuring that pupils know what bullying is and what to do if it happens. Pupils are comfortable with the idea of asking adults for help to sort things out. The school has excellent arrangements for child protection. They build on the pupils' feelings of being safe and cared for by school routines. The school is outstandingly successful in promoting the health, safety and general well-being of its pupils.

Partnership with parents and the community

The school has very good links with the great majority of its parents. It has very effective partnerships with those whose pupils have complex special educational needs. Staff have worked very hard to develop good relationships with parents and wider families. Parents are involved in the life and work of the school in different ways. They help regularly in classrooms, on visits and with particular projects.

Parents are fully involved in reviews of statements of special educational needs. They are strongly encouraged to share their views and experiences of the child's progress. This helps to develop a real sense of partnership which is used to support the child's learning and development. The quality of genuine teamwork, involving parents, staff and people from other agencies is very impressive.

The school's work is enriched by links with the local community which make a strong contribution to the effective life of the school. The school has its own very strong sense of community which is particularly good at making all the pupils feel valued.

Support, guidance and pupils' welfare

Teachers, support staff and adult volunteers have very good working relationships. These help to create an atmosphere where pupils' well-being can be nurtured and supported positively. The

Appendix 2: Extracts from the 1998 OFSTED Report

staff provide a safe environment in which all pupils can feel secure. There are pupils in Year 3 who respond well to the opportunity to tackle challenging puzzles in mathematics. Because they receive high quality support from teachers, the pupils feel comfortable about taking the risk of learning from their mistakes. This is having a positive effect on the standards they achieve. The youngest pupils are helped to settle into school life by effective arrangements. The pupils take part in preschool visits so that by the time they start school they know a range of familiar, friendly faces.

The school provides good support and guidance for its pupils although there are weaknesses in the arrangements for assessing and monitoring their academic progress that limit the quality of support they are given. By contrast, pupils with special educational needs benefit from systems which track what they know, understand and can do. For instance, annual reviews make good use of the individual education plans and show careful observations and records of signs of progress. These enable the school and parents to work together on specific targets to support further development. Pupils with special educational needs are supported very well within teaching groups. Support assistants do all they can, together with other pupils in the class, to ensure that those with special educational needs, however complex, can join in the everyday activities in the school.

Appendix 3

The Newham LEA Inclusion Charter and extracts from the Audit

Introduction

This document has been developed by Project Inclusion, working with parents, teachers, head teachers, children and young people. The Audit is based on the good practice that is happening in Newham schools. The points have been developed through interviews and observation. A consultation exercise on a draft audit was carried out, again involving parents, SENCOs, learning support staff, primary and secondary head teachers. Part of the consultation exercise was trialing the audit in selected schools. It is hoped the Inclusive Education Audit will help schools examine their development towards providing Inclusive Education. It has been designed to be a working document so that schools can identify their own priorities.

The document begins with the Inclusive Education Charter launched in November 1997. The elements of the Charter are broken down into points of good practice. There is room on each page to add additional points so that the Audit will become an individual school document. It is hoped that the points added will be incorporated into any future updating.

We aim to have structures and policies that promote inclusion, covering:

- a policy of making all parents and carers feel their children will be welcomed and supported at the school;
- a policy of welcoming and doing our best to meet the needs of all children and young people attending the school, whatever special educational needs or disability they have;
- governors and staff who are trained in disability awareness issues;
- a policy that ensures recruitment and training of staff who will support and are committed to inclusion;
- an inclusion policy that is an integral part of the school development plan;
- a special needs policy that is rigorously implemented and reviewed.

Appendix 3: The Newham LEA Inclusion Charter and extracts from the Audit

We aim to promote high levels of achievement for all children and young people by:

- offering a wide range of learning and teaching experiences;
- developing and implementing Individual Education Plans for children and young people with special educational needs;
- valuing the contribution of all children and young people;
- having high expectations of all children and young people;
- training staff to equip them to teach all children and young people.

We aim to include all children and young people in all the activities of the school by:

- fostering supportive friendships among children and young people;
- having clear codes of behaviour that take account of the particular difficulties that certain children and young people face;
- working to enable children and young people to become more independent;
- finding ways to overcome any difficulties caused by the physical environment, school rules or routines;
- promoting diversity, understanding difficulties, recognising and respecting individual differences;
- taking positive steps to prevent exclusions, especially of children and young people with statements of special educational needs.

We aim to work in partnership with parents and carers by:

- welcoming parents and carers into the school;
- making written and spoken language accessible;
- dealing with parents and carers with honesty, trust and discretion;
- taking time, sharing information, listening to and valuing contributions in meetings.

Why do we want children and young people with disabilities and other difficulties to be educated with everyone else?

a. Because there are benefits for all children and young people:

- It gives them a larger range of social experiences and greater awareness and sensitivity towards the difficulties of other children.
- It shows them there can be something positive about being different.
- Children become more accepting and supporting of each other and they value each other.
- It helps them to come to terms with the things which they find difficult themselves; children with disabilities can be role models for others.
- It puts them in a situation where they can learn something practical about human rights.

The parents' support groups have their own room in the school

- If all children go to school in their own neighbourhood, it means their school is genuinely comprehensive.
- It helps the whole-school community to get used to solving problems jointly by small steps and not just waiting for long-term outcomes.

b. Because there are benefits for the children and young people with disabilities:

- It helps them to become more mature and independent.
- It gives them role models for social behaviour and improves their language development.
- It gives them access to a wider range of lessons and experiences.
- Children have the opportunity to join the real world, because they will have to do so when they are older.
- It gives them a feeling that they have something to offer to other children and that their contribution is valued.

c. Because there are benefits for the whole community:

- Today's children are tomorrow's parents, and can learn about the variety of experiences that parents have.
- Today's children are also tomorrow's architects, planners and politicians, and their own experience of inclusion will help them to create a non-segregated environment.
- As barriers of ignorance are broken down, the community can become more supportive and aware of children's difficulties.
- If schools are a central part of the community and all children are part of the community from the beginning, society will have a true picture of itself.
- In a multicultural area, inclusion of children with disabilities helps people to become more aware of the different cultures of their fellow citizens.

Appendix 3: The Newham LEA Inclusion Charter and extracts from the Audit

The Audit

The Audit, which, in the full document, follows the Charter, takes each aim in turn and breaks it down into questions to help schools to assess how they are practising inclusion. Here are some examples.

1. *Including all children and young people in all the activities of the school; fostering supportive friendships among children and young people*

- supporting new groupings in school and challenging groups which exclude others because of gender, race or disability;
- taking into account friendship and support groupings when deciding teaching groups for children and young people;
- creating a sense of membership of a tutor group or class group and supporting this;
- enhancing children's and young people's understanding of each other;
- empowering children and young people to support each other when victims of discrimination or bullying;
- incorporating discussions about friendships, self-esteem, etc. into curriculum time;
- organising activities that facilitate friendships within peer groups and across the age range;
- using peers as a resource for including others;
- having clear procedures for reporting and dealing constructively with prejudice from other children and young people;
- ensuring that all pupils have the opportunity, if they choose, to attend after-school clubs;
- helping children and young people to understand their own disability or difficulty and to have the language to explain to others;
- promoting an environment where disability issues can be discussed by children, young people and adults;
- encouraging classmates to take responsibility at break times;
- examining how children and young people work and play together and how friendship can be fostered.

2. *Having clear codes of behaviour that take account of the particular difficulties that certain children face*

- a behaviour code that ensures respect for all members of the community;
- a behaviour code that can respond to the needs of individual children and young people;
- a behaviour code that can respond effectively to challenging behaviour;
- a behaviour code that is seen as fair by staff and children and young people;
- a behaviour code that has expectations for adults as well as children and young people;

- a behaviour code that can respond to children and young people who have emotional and behavioural difficulties;
- a recognition that different children and young people may respond positively to different approaches;
- opportunities to discuss expectations of behaviour;
- having clear information about counselling and other external services that are available to children and young people;
- involving the disruptive child or young person in developing strategies to manage behaviour;
- avoiding unnecessary physical management of children and young people.

3. *Working to enable children and young people to become more independent*

- recognising the importance of working independently;
- validating the child's or young person's own experiences and resources within the learning process;
- involving the students in problem-solving approaches in both academic and pastoral issues;
- recognising the importance of independence and life skills work in Personal, Health and Social Education;
- recognising and responding to the social needs of children and young people;
- including targets in independence in Individual Education Plans;
- using support staff to develop independence;
- monitoring the work of the learning support assistants and working to decrease one-to-one support whenever possible;
- celebrating the child's or young person's initiative;
- examining progress towards independence at review;
- recognising the importance of having time to work alone and with friends for all children and young people;
- offering age-appropriate activities;
- offering choices that are age-appropriate;
- interacting with the child or young person in a manner consistent with their chronological age.

4. *Finding ways to overcome any difficulties caused by the physical environment, school rules or routines*

- monitoring the causes of a child's or young person's difficulties;
- monitoring the antecedents and contexts of temporary and permanent exclusions;
- offering alternatives to large playgrounds, busy entrances, long periods of similar activities, etc. if they are of clear benefit to the child or young person;
- working with the LEA to overcome any structural difficulties;
- admitting children and young people who may have toileting difficulties;
- planning of all transitions (between activities/lessons) carefully;

- finding ways to include all children and young people on school trips;
- ensuring the child or young person is included during any absence of a support assistant.

5. *Promoting diversity, understanding difficulties, recognising and respecting individual differences*

- using language that is not racist, sexist or insulting to people who have disabilities;
- providing an environment where inappropriate language or behaviour can be challenged;
- using resources that promote positive images of disability;
- auditing equipment regularly to ensure resources do not present negative stereotypes;
- ensuring that issues of disability equality are understood by staff, children and young people;
- ensuring that the school policy has clear procedures to follow when there is inappropriate language and/or behaviour;
- challenging assumptions/stereotypes about disability;
- avoiding highlighting children and young people because of their disabilities or other difficulties;
- avoiding thinking that all difficulties have to be cured rather than accepted and understood;
- accepting only positive images/language in informal settings, staff room, parents' room.

6. *Taking positive steps to prevent exclusions, especially of young people with statements of special educational need*

- recognising that children and young people may benefit from changes to support arrangements, groupings, timetables, etc.;
- following local authority guidelines and seeking appropriate help and guidance;
- distributing guidelines to all staff on preventing exclusions;
- facilitating meetings to prevent exclusions;
- ensuring staff have clear behaviour management guidelines for individual children or young people who may need them.

7. *Working in partnership with parents and carers; welcoming parents and carers into the school*

- ensuring the building is accessible;
- creating regular opportunities for formal and informal contact;
- recognising the vast knowledge and experience of parents and carers;
- creating an area in school that is available for parents' and carers' use;
- holding up-to-date information for parents and carers on advocacy, helplines, etc.;
- ensuring all staff have a welcoming and courteous manner.

Bibliography

Ainscow, M. (1995) 'Special needs through school improvement', in Clark, C., Dyson, A., Millward, A. (eds) *Towards Inclusive Schools?* 63–77. London: David Fulton Publishers.

Alderson, P. (ed.) (1997) *Changing Our School: Promoting Positive Behaviour.* London: Institute of Education and Plymouth: Highfield School.

Alderson, P. and Goodey, C. (1998) *Enabling Education: Experiences in Special and Ordinary Schools.* London: Tufnell Press.

Armstrong, D. (1995) *Power and Partnership in Education.* London: Routledge.

Audit Commission/HMI (1992) *Getting in on the Act.* London: HMSO.

Ayers, H., Clarke, D., Murray, A. (1995) *Perspectives on Behaviour: A Practical Guide to Effective Interventions for Teachers.* London: David Fulton Publishers.

Beane, J. (1990) *Affect in the Curriculum: Towards Democracy, Dignity and Diversity.* New York: Teacher College, Columbia University.

Booth, T. (1996) 'Changing views of research on integration: the inclusion of students with "special needs" or participation for all?' in Sigston, A., Curran, P., Labram, A., Wolfendale, S. (eds) *Psychology in Practice with Young People, Families and Schools.* London: David Fulton Publishers.

Clough, P. and Barton, L. (1995) *Making Difficulties: Research and the Construction of Special Educational Needs.* London: Paul Chapman.

Cornwall, J. (1997) *Access to Learning for Pupils with Disabilities.* London: David Fulton Publishers.

Department for Education and Employment (1997a). *Excellence in Schools.* London: HMSO.

Department for Education and Employment (1997b) *Excellence for all Children: Meeting Special Educational Needs.* London: HMSO.

Department for Education and Employment (1997) *The SENCO Guide.* London: HMSO.

Dessent, T. (1987) *Making the Ordinary School Special.* London: Falmer Press.

Finch, S. (1998) *'An Eye for an Eye Leaves Everyone Blind': Teaching Young Children to Settle Conflicts without Violence. A Handbook for Early Years Workers.* London: National Early Years Network/ Save the Children.

Galloway, D., Armstrong, D., Tomlinson, S. (1994) *The Assessment of Special Educational Needs: Whose Problem?* London: Longman.

Gardner, H. (1993) *The Unschooled Mind: How Children Think and How Schools Should Teach.* London: Fontana.

Griffith, R. (1998) *Educational Citizenship and Independent Learning.* London: Jessica Kingsley Publishers.

Hurley, N. (1998) *Straight Talk: Working with Children and Young People in Groups.* York: Joseph Rowntree Foundation.

Lewis, A. (1995a) *Children's Understanding of Disability.* London: Routledge.

Lewis, A. (1995b) *Primary Special Needs and the National Curriculum.* London: Routledge.

McNamara, S. and Moreton, G. (1993) *Teaching Special Needs.* London: David Fulton Publishers.

McNamara, S. and Moreton, G. (1995) *Changing Behaviour: Teaching Children with Emotional and Behavioural Difficulties in Primary and Secondary Classrooms.* London: David Fulton Publishers.

McNamara, S. and Moreton, G. (1997) *Understanding Differentiation: A Teacher's Guide.* London: David Fulton Publishers.

Miller, J. (1996) *Never Too Young: How Young Children Can Take Responsibility and Make Decisions. A Handbook for Early Years Workers.* London: National Early Years Network/ Save the Children.

Morris, J. (1998) *Don't Leave Us Out: Involving Disabled Children and Young People with Communication Impairments.* York: Joseph Rowntree Foundation.

Mosley, J. (1993) *Turn Your School Round.* Wisbech: LDA.

Newham Local Education Authority (1997) *Inclusive Education Charter and Audit.* London: Newham LEA.

Newham Local Education Authority (1998) *Guide to the Literacy Hour.* London: Newham LEA.

Pfister, M. (1996) *The Rainbow Fish.* Zurich: Nord-Sud-Verlag AG.

Sammons, P., Hillman, M., Mortimore, P. (1995) *Key Characteristics of Effective Schools.* London: Office for Standards in Education.

UNESCO (1994) *Declaration of World Conference on Special Educational Needs (The Salamanca Ddeclaration).* Paris: UNESCO.

United Nations (1989) *Convention on the Rights of the Child.* Geneva: UN.

Ward, L. (1997) *Seen and Heard: Involving Disabled Children and Young People in Research and Development Projects.* York: Joseph Rowntree Foundation.

For Product Safety Concerns and Information please contact our EU representative GPSR@taylorandfrancis.com
Taylor & Francis Verlag GmbH, Kaufingerstraße 24, 80331 München, Germany